Through a Country Window

Other Books by Eric E. Wright:

Tell the World
Church—No Spectator Sport
Strange Fire?

Through A Country Window

*Inspiring Stories from Out
Where the Sky Springs Free*

PUBLISHING

Belleville, Ontario, Canada

Through a Country Window
Copyright © 2001, Eric E. Wright

National Library of Canada Cataloguing in Publication Data

Wright, Eric E., 1935-
. Through a country window : inspiring stories from out where the sky springs free

Includes index.
ISBN: 1-55306-202-7

1. Country life – Ontario – Hope (Township) – Anecdotes. I. Title.

FC3095.H652Z49 2001   971.3'56   C2001-930029-8
F1059.H66W74 2001

Essence Publishing is a Christian Book Publisher dedicated to furthering the work of Christ through the written word. For more information, contact: 44 Moira Street West, Belleville, Ontario, Canada K8P 1S3.
Phone: 1-800-238-6376. Fax: (613) 962-3055.
E-mail: info@essencegroup.com
Internet: www.essencegroup.com

Printed in Canada
by

Essence
PUBLISHING

For
Mary Helen
my country soul-mate

Table of Contents

Spring

 ## Summer

Sorrow and Celebration

Acknowledgements

The rural countryside of Northumberland County, and the people who live there, must be credited for providing the rich strands of colour I've woven into this country tapestry.

I appreciate the encouragement of Stephen and Catherine, Deborah and Brian, John and Shona.

Shareena, Adrianna, and Kassandra, three nearby grand-daughters, have helped to make some of our rural adventures especially memorable.

Sharon Cavers and Stephen Kennedy, core members of my local writers' support group, have been unflagging in their enthusiasm. Their input has been of immeasurable help in correcting grammar, spelling, and in giving advice over a period of several years.

Thanks to Norm, my brother, for giving me a final push to publish.

Without Mary Helen, my country companion, lifelong helpmate, and best friend, who has shared every minute of our country dream, read every word dozens of times, and whose interaction has been indispensable, there would have been no country dream.

Of course, without our gracious Creator, there would be no singing sky, no honking geese, no winking stars, no changing seasons.

Quotations have been selected for their individual merit and do not necessarily reflect my agreement with the philosophy of their authors.

Most neighbours have been fictionalized to preserve their anonymity.

COUNTRY INITIATION

Prologue—Country Search

Our doubts are traitors,
and make us lose the good
we oft might win
by fearing to attempt.[1]

I n 1991, we laid aside our doubts. I quit my full-time job, and we embraced our dream of moving to the country from our suburban home in Toronto. Soon, however, our careful plan was in tatters. City real estate hit the skids. The part-time jobs I had counted on fell through. Savings evaporated. With growing frustration, we surveyed the best part of a hundred country properties until we discovered a gem. A year that seriously tested our resolution gyrated wildly by before we could make the move.

The chapters ahead tell of the pleasure and pitfalls we discovered along the way. They recount our awakening delight in scenes observed through our country window: the moon rising, the leaves turning, the snow falling, the geese returning in the spring. They also describe some of the lessons we are learning, for the countryside in which we live is not only a delightful environment; it is our school, our laboratory, and our cathedral. It has become an integral part of our lives. We cannot now imagine living away from the rolling hills of Northumberland, beyond the spring-fed valleys, out from under the arc of the heavens, beyond the sight of wind-blown pines.

Appreciation for nature takes us deeper than the momentary delight we find in a pleasing scene, for the countryside is not just scenery. Joseph Wood Krutch, writing of his experience in the Arizona desert, says it well.

> *Scenery, as such, never meant much to me.... Then, having lived somewhat unwillingly in a quiet countryside for a year and a half, I made the great and obvious discovery which thousands must have made before me. There is all the difference in the world between looking at something and living with it. In nature, one never really sees a thing for the first time until one has seen it for the fiftieth. It never means much until it has become part of some general configuration, until it has become not a 'view' or a 'sight' but an integrated world of which one is a part.[2]*

Country living, of course, involves far more than nature. It encompasses the characters who people the villages and farms: the old couple rattling slowly by in their ancient pickup; Lev on his combine; the local sun worshipper parading around in a thong; the mad motorcyclist; the owner of the village store; the fire brigade volunteers; Fudge with his working gristmill; many salt-of-the-earth neighbours. What would country living be without characters? Although most are real, I have fictionalized some neighbours to preserve their anonymity.

"Country," in this corner of Ontario, also means maple syrup time, spring plowing, small-town parades, outdoor theatre, fall fairs, harvest, snowmobile races, and gossip—lots of gossip at the country store.

Although this story takes place in the Northumberland Hills east of Toronto, our experiences will resonate with all who love country life, whether they live in the Smokies east of Knoxville or in the Yorkshire Dales north of London. Our experiences are shared by others in widely scattered places around the earth. Mountains, seacoast, arctic, desert, jungle, prairies, steppes, forests, and pampas; each kind of topography has its own brand of beauty. The Creator's art is on display everywhere.

Our narrative begins in late August and continues through the seasons. Autumn was the first full season we enjoyed after moving into Hemlock Meadow, as we came to call our home. The logs and beams are Hemlock, cut from a local bush.

There is another reason, however, to begin our narrative with late summer and early autumn. Too much modern writing is gloomy and pessimistic, describing the human condition by the metaphor of winter—cold, deadly, and unforgiving. In our experience, such a view is neither true to the beauties peculiar to winter nor sensitive to life as it can be lived. Winter is not the end. Every season prepares for the next.

There is no season such delight can bring,
As summer, autumn, winter, and the spring.[3]

Gossip Central

Security is mostly superstition.
It does not exist in nature.
Life is either a daring adventure
or nothing.[4]

The chirp of one tiny cricket woke me on the morning after our big move. Groggily I looked around. Piles of boxes, two and three deep, littered the room. Every muscle in my body ached. Stiff from sleeping on a mattress flung on the floor, I could tell by the sunlight dancing off the polished pine that we had overslept. Then I heard it again.

Poking Mary Helen, I whispered, "Did you hear that cricket?"

"Huh-h?" she yawned. "Whew! Glad you woke me. I was having a nightmare. Piles of boxes in a dirty warehouse. We couldn't find our way out!"

Mary Helen's dream adventures in the land of Morpheus are enough to fill a book. This book, however, is about a different kind of dream—the dream of finding a log house on an acre or two of grass and trees in a country setting without going broke; the dream of exchanging streetlights for starlight; the dream of finding a place that would inspire the muse.

Helen Keller encourages us to choose adventure over security. A year earlier, we had chosen adventure. But the shredding of all our carefully-laid plans had sorely tested our resolve. With housing sales in the cellar, a succession of "For Sale" signs from an assortment of realtors yielded nothing but a procession of the curious who tracked dirt over our clean floors and poked in our closets. We couldn't move and expenses mounted. Fortunately, Mary Helen's craft business helped keep us afloat. Customers clamoured for her designer baskets.

Although frustration often withered our hopes during that year-long wait, they kept reappearing like shoots on a willow stump. For one thing, a publisher expressed interest in a book I had just completed. For another, we frequently jumped in the car and headed for open country. Being out there beyond the concrete, with a view of forest-fringed fields and singing streams, beneath the immensity of the sky, quickly restored our blighted hopes.

The chirp of the cricket broke through my reverie. Mary Helen heard it too; "Eric, there's a cricket in the bedroom! Get it!"

"I hear others answering from downstairs. Isn't this great. We're really in the country!"

"Are you crazy? Find it! I can't stand bugs in the bedroom!"

"Did we pack any insect spray?" I yawned as I groped for my slippers.

Tossing a magazine at the offending critter, she whispered, "No! Just get those bugs."

"First I need coffee. Where's the coffee maker?"

"In the big box marked linens," she mumbled, as she pulled the sheet over her head and drifted back to sleep.

At our bedroom door I stopped to glance down the hall toward the room with the skylights, where I would set up my office. Descending the stairs to the front door, I basked in the sunshine streaming through the front window before continuing down the staircase to the sunken main floor. Turning toward the kitchen, I began my search. Dishes, pots, cutlery, and bags of groceries covered the kitchen counter. Paper plates and pizza boxes overflowing from a garbage bag were the only signs of the family and friends who had helped us move the day before.

I paused to gaze around at the honey-coloured log walls, the massive posts and beams holding up the thick pine planks of the upper floor, and the wood stove nestled in the corner. It was hard to believe I was not dreaming, but caffeine withdrawal soon brought me back to the task at hand.

"Why would anyone pack the coffee percolator in a box marked 'linens'?" I grumbled as I manhandled boxes.

I finally found the percolator in with the pillowcases, but where, oh where, had Mary Helen hidden the coffee? It was fifteen miles to the nearest supermarket. A lingering worry skated around the edge of my mind. We were a long way from the city and all our friends. We didn't know our neighbours. And by this time I heard crickets chirping from the laundry room, the living room, and from under the pile of furniture in the corner of the dining room. What had we done? Had we invested in a cricket condo?

"We must've been crazy to move into a house in the middle of nowhere," I mumbled.

Obviously, I needed some java. Returning upstairs, I struggled into my pants and woke Mary Helen again to tell her, "There's no coffee, but I'll see if that little store in the village has any."

"Eggs too," she groaned rather incoherently.

As we quickly discovered, every respectable village has a general store. Garden Hill's sits on the south side of the county road, across from a barnyard and some fields that encircle the old church with its lofty steeple. Driving up, I negotiated a space in the midst of a pack of pick-ups and 4 x 4s that crowded the shoulder, signaling what counts as bustle in Garden Hill.

Asbestos shingles, that were the rage in the late '40s, camouflaged the two-story relic's scars. Four weathered timbers propped up a sagging porch roof. A brand-new steel door made the whole structure look like the cratered face of an old-timer with one gold tooth.

A sign swung in the breeze proudly proclaiming, "Garden Hill General Store." To the right of the door, an ice machine and a bank of army-green mailboxes leaned dejectedly against the wall. To the left, past the empty racks that had been used months ago to sell spring bedding plants, a shed full of cobwebs and debris leaned east. "Bull Pen—Video Games," declared the sign over the missing door. The work of an earlier entrepreneur, the shed waited silently for its appointment with high-tech success. A shiny new phone booth sat, proud and aloof, in front of the store.

The windows on either side of the store's steel door told a livelier tale. Posters and notices plastered the lower third of the windows: a corn roast put on by the fire brigade, a craft show in Millbrook, a new play by the Fourth Line Theatre, a farm auction.

This artifact was not on the list of local tourist attractions. What slowed tourists barreling east to prime fishing on Rice Lake was not the speed limit. No, it was more likely kids cranky for ice cream and pop, or hungry for fries available at the chip truck parked beside the store throughout the spring, summer, and fall.

To walk inside, however, was to be transported, Alice-like through the looking glass, into another time and place. The tinkling of a bell signaled my entrance. A neighbouring farmer stood inside, sipping coffee. He wore faded green coveralls and a red flannel shirt with the sleeves rolled up to reveal corded forearms. At six-foot-something, his wrestler physique radiated brute strength. Tufts of black hair stuck out from under a Co-op cap.

Sporting several days' stubble, Gary, the owner, was working the lottery terminal for a bull-necked farmer half a head shorter than the wrestler prototype. Gary's eyebrows lifted expressively, up and down, up and down, as he emphasized a point—something about a grass fire.

"Just about reached my barn," snorted a grizzled farmer in coveralls. "Another ten minutes and—poof!"

"Real dry. No rain in weeks," responded a younger man draped over the counter. "Dangerous."

"Lucky it happened when the volunteers were at home," interjected Gary. "Bad news if it had caught when they were all at work."

I tried to catch the conversation without seeming to listen. I could feel them eyeing my stiff new jeans and discarding me as "nouveau-country." Stifling my interest in the talk of fire, I threaded my way past shelves of soup, beans, tuna, and cereal. The worn boards creaked as I skirted the sagging trap-door in the floor to get at the cooler full of local brown eggs, butter, cheese, milk, and—strangely enough—Cool Whip.

Later, I learned that Gary and his petite wife, Cathy, who takes her shift in the store, were not locals. When the fields around the village where they grew up disappeared before the juggernaut of "progress," Gary and Cathy bought the Garden Hill Store. They wanted their growing family to enjoy the wide-open space they remembered as children.

Ten years later, the store continues to be the centre of a communications network that beats Ma Bell and e-mail hands down. Gary has the answers. Where the deer are yarding—"south of Nine along Beaver Meadow Road;" why the fire truck was up in Thomsville that last winter Saturday—"a bad snowmobile accident... one man with a bloody gash... ambulance got stuck... had to call the volunteer fire brigade for help;" what the man was doing with a shotgun and dogs along Trespass Road the other day—"either rabbits or coyotes. Been some coyotes around your place last winter."

From motor oil to mayonnaise, coffee to cold cuts, Gary carries whatever you need. One whole annex is chock-full of staples for evening entertainment; pop, chips, cheesies, and up-to-date videos. An old-fashioned cooler displays a few stalks of celery, green peppers, lettuce, some tomatoes, and an assortment of cold meats, including what I learned was a perennial favourite, pepperoni sticks.

Below a yellowing picture of the store in its heyday and one of Gary holding up a massive muskie, a rack displays a wide range of magazines. Another holds newspapers, reserved by name, for people from all over the area. Every available space on the bulletin board is plastered with business cards, announcements, requests for employment, notices of wood for sale, and even the offer of a foot nurse, whatever that might be.

As I headed toward the front with my eggs and coffee, I overheard Gary chatting with the farmer whose barn nearly caught fire. "Yeah, he was having a coffee when his beeper went off. Called all the other guys from here and got to your place fast."

"Sure glad it wasn't like last year when he responded to that chimney fire," Gary continued. "On the way to the fire, he lost control and drove that new engine into the ditch."

During a lull in the conversation, I interjected, "Hi, I'm the new owner of the Austen place up on Trespass Road. Would you have any insect spray?"

To my astonishment Gary responded, "You're Mr. Wright aren't you? I deliver the mail; that's why I know your name. Over there on the top shelf."

We learned later that, until the store developed a strong clientele, Gary moonlighted from time to time. During our first few years, he had the contract to deliver mail. Snow, sleet, rain, hail, ice, fog—no problem, he came through. Then someone outbid his tender. It must have become hard to feed his growing family on the profit from the store, although lottery tickets and cigarettes probably helped.

A few years ago, Gary dug up the registry files going back to 1858, when Garden Hill had three water-driven mills. His commemorative mugs, featuring the store, show him as the eighteenth owner to continue its "tradition of serving the community." Beside the mugs, T-shirts advertise, "University of Garden Hill." Not a bad caption—country wisdom is not to be scorned.

In 1935, the original store and several surrounding houses burned to the ground when a neighbour with electric lights spilled gas on his hot generator. Could there be something symbolic in the fact that I was born that year?

In the city, I never quite got into the convenience store scene. Those who ran the ones in our neighbourhood seemed more interested in my wallet than my family. They were community stores with little sense of community. The Garden Hill store is different. It's an institution, an integral part of village social life, part of a vibrant rural community. People stop as much to sip coffee and gossip as to buy. They know each other's names and a whole lot more: who just had a baby; whose grandfather needs an operation; the score of the local ball team; the six-point buck that crossed the road near highway twenty-eight; where to find a good electrician.

Over the years, we've come to rely on Gary. "Gary, what's a good spy video?" Often as not, he'd recommend a winner. "Gary, do you have any paraffin wax? We ran out in the middle of canning!" "Sure. Down the aisle on the left, bottom shelf, near the back." "Gary, do you have any two-stroke engine oil for my lawnmower?" "Right by the window." "Gary, do you know anyone who can repair a microwave?" "Try that fix-it shop in town."

This is no flashy supermarket, no multi-national moneymaker, but it is a focal point of community life. And a sense of community is one of the most attractive features of living in the country.

There is "a growing sense of longing in society, …not so much a longing for what was as it is for what could be. It is, in essence, a longing for community."[5]

To some people, community is a feeling,
to some people, it's relationships,
to some people it's a place,

to some people it's an institution.
[But I prefer to define it as] a place where people prevail.[6]

Crazy Crickets

The cricket's gone, we only hear machines;
In erg and atom they exact their pay.
And life is largely lived on silver screens.[7]

C rickets can drive you crazy. As the summer waned, cricket legions viewed our cozy home as an ideal winter retreat. Instead of a frontal attack, they infiltrated. They raided the cupboards, invaded the cutlery drawer, set up garrisons behind the furniture, assailed the bathrooms, stormed the bedrooms and… well, you get the picture.

No need for Mozart. Cricket ensembles serenaded us from every corner. Whenever we snuck up on a soloist, its score read *sotto voce*, while its companion on the opposite side of the room played *forte*. We tiptoed in absolute silence, but the thump of our hearts and the gurgling of our tummies must have warned them of our approach. When we did discover a culprit, our thunderous attack provoked a dirge from the rest of the orchestra.

We fell asleep to a cricket concerto. We woke to a cricket med-
ley. One morning we traced a particularly melodic violinist to a
teacup we had decoratively hung on the wall. "Look at that cheeky
little thing," I huffed. "Well, at least we've caught another."

"Eric, you've got to do something," directed my sweet naturalist rather indignantly. "Nature is wonderful but let's keep it
outside!"

Nature, I recalled, had attracted us to this area in the first
place. I remembered the day we first drove down Trespass Road
to view a log house nestled among pines. It was one of those
uncertain days in March that could go either way—another wild
snowstorm or a final thaw. As we crested a rise for a glance at the
last prospect of the day, a fox darted across the road in front of
us—wildlife running free!

The waning days of winter had made us restless to push on
with our search. We would set out on a Saturday morning in
high hopes with a list of four or five properties. At first, we wandered the rolling hills north and west of the city. Soon we discovered that those luscious miles of picture-perfect horse farms,
golf courses, and woodlots were reserved for bankers, lawyers,
and those who had money socked away in offshore accounts.

Ranging farther afield, we visited Victorian farmhouses with
primitive wiring; a pioneer reproduction deep in maple woods
with floors so authentic the cracks would swallow a Pekinese
without a trace; century-old log homes with patches that suspi-
ciously looked like dry rot; brick bungalows and vinyl-sided
Cape Cods. We had pictures of houses everywhere. Before our
odyssey came to an end, we had visited more than 100 homes
within a hundred-mile radius of the city.

We soon caught on to real estate jargon. "Handy man's spe
cial" meant the house would collapse under the next heavy
snow. "Gardener's delight" was a cover for a house set down on

acres of barren clay with not a tree in sight. One agent insisted, after showing us a comfortable house in a field of mud, that all we needed to do was transplant some big trees. "Not with our budget and a limited lifespan," we murmured.

By now, the romance of log homes held us firmly in its grip. Friends looked at us strangely as we passed around pictures and explained, "This is scribed Scandinavian style and that one is milled log with dovetail corners. Now this one here is Quebec style with chinking." Which is why we happened to be on Trespass Road that Saturday.

The folder describing the log house quoted a price well beyond our reach. But, well, we couldn't resist at least driving by. We pulled over to the side of the road and rolled down the window. Boulders lined the gravel drive down to the two-car garage. White chinking set off each huge log in the main structure and a double door invited entry to the warmth within. Lawns surrounded the home on three sides while pines and giant oaks framed the house from behind. I could easily imagine myself soaking up the sun on the deck that peeked out from under the wide gables on the right.

This one had it all; a couple of acres with lawns where we could enjoy the summer sun, woods to shelter the house from winter gales, and a country setting to inspire the muse. I picked up the real estate profile and read aloud, "Four bedrooms. Open concept. Bright cathedral living room. Pine cupboards in the kitchen. Two bathrooms. Honey, we better put this one out of our minds completely."

"And almost two acres," Mary Helen responded, "But so much money!"

"Well, no harm in a picture," I said as I framed the log vision in the viewfinder of my battered Yashica.

Mary Helen tossed the data sheet carelessly onto the back

seat on top of all the others. I put the car in gear and headed home. This particular fantasy would go to the bottom of our list of possibilities.

Our fantasy, although realized, had not included crickets. Foxes and deer, yes. Crickets and flies, no. But what to do? Crickets seemed to have taken up residence behind the baseboard in the walls.

In our determination to destroy all their hiding places, we went a little crazy that first year. We ripped up the quarter round and pulled back the carpet on the main floor. After spraying insecticide along the innards thus exposed, I tried to seal any crevices with caulking compound. What a miserable job. To make sure I left no niche for crickets, I had to lie on my side much of the time while sweat dripped in my eyes. Not being an artist with a caulking gun, I made a huge mess. Caulking on the rug. Caulking on the baseboard. Too much here, too little there. The pros spit on their fingers to smooth it out—which I imitated—but ended up with caulking all over my hands and on my nose. I did succeed in entombing a number of the invaders.

It wasn't until later that we learned the previous owner had kept a dog in the mud room at the back. The open door gave the crickets leave to march their battalions into strategic positions in the mud room. There they formed into platoons waiting for the order to "charge" from the sentries they posted at our sliding doors. Whenever we opened these doors, they whispered, "Go! Go! Go!" We were invaded right under our noses. The next year, we were much more vigilant when crickets received their "inside call" in late summer.

Nowadays we are old country hands. The odd cricket that passes our defenses is more amusing than maddening.

Not all our insect adventures have been so successful. As fall approached, dozens of flies mysteriously appeared on the inside of our windows and skylights. A few even materialized between the panes of our double-glazed windows. They buzzed in lazy circles back and forth—stupid cousins of the more agile house fly. Where did they come from? How did they get in? Even after carefully scooping up every fly, they came back as numerous as ever. Were they spontaneously generating before our very eyes?

Mary Helen took to bounding from window to window with weapon in hand. After sucking up the invaders from one window with her portable vacuum, she would charge to the next battlefield. But rather than subject them to a cruel death, her tender heart compelled her to release them outside. Strange behaviour for a farm girl!

"Honey, they'll just find another way to come in if you don't kill them," I expostulated.

When heavy frost imprisoned the fields, the flies diminished, only to appear again whenever the temperature rose. As winter advanced, the invaders disappeared altogether except for the odd one that would circle out of nowhere just when we were entertaining city friends for dinner.

The following year, I learned the secret of the cluster flies from a pest control flyer in the mailbox. Every year several generations germinate in the soil. The final generation before winter seeks a warm place to hibernate by clustering together at cracks and crevices along windows, doors, and eaves where heat leaks from a house. They squeeze through impossible spaces in their search for warmth.

There is not much I can do about them unless I go hyper about sealing every teensy crevice. So every fall, I prepare myself for fall fever—the season in which Mary Helen goes a little balmy for a few weeks.

Country living has its little nuisances. If it's not crickets or flies, it's manure. Nothing I can do about that, either. We live in the country, but so do cows and pigs and horses and goats and chickens and lots of others. Fortunately, the aroma is unnoticeable except when Lev spatters his fields in the spring. To many transplanted urbanites, however, the rich farm smell is an infringement on their right to life, liberty, and the pursuit of happiness—life without bad smells, liberty from stench, and the pursuit of the blissful scent of lilac and roses.

As the millennium turned over, people were raising a stink. The issue had become so serious in Minnesota that a university there sought specialists to work for three years on a program designed to set an "odour emissions rating system" for the state's feedlots. Soon a panel of 35 sniffers was hard at work categorizing the components of cow and pig manure in order to develop a 'formal state stench test'.[8] The cost? $390,000!

This kind of palaver doesn't just occur in our neighbour to the south. Farmers and environmentalists have clashed in the Quebec legislature over rural noise, dust, and odours. And John Locke, of the Alberta Environmental Network, charged that Canada's growing pig industry was turning us into a stinking "bacon republic"![9]

Recently, this issue aroused our sleepy little township to full cry. Pressure to allow more intensive pig farms in the area created a storm of opposition. In porcine factories, thousands of pigs are confined in tiny spaces for their entire lives. Besides institutionalizing cruelty, these operations release enormous amounts of waste into the surrounding environment. Fortunately, restrictions were enforced.

Life has its irritations. In the country we have crickets, mosquitoes, cluster flies, poison ivy and sometimes, odours. City folk have to put up with noise, lineups, traffic, and smog. Both of us have skunks and raccoons. We both get colds and the flu. All of us have to endure bureaucracy.

We came to the country with the rather idealized intention of recreating some kind of Walden. The crickets and flies and smells quickly reminded us that we live east of Eden where "sins and sorrows grow and thorns infest the ground." But hey, country aggravations can be beneficial. They force us to face our imperfections—that we tend to get annoyed at foolish things, that we are too often frustrated by minor inconveniences. They help us to eat humble pie in private so we can avoid demonstrating our insufferable arrogance in public.

Serenading crickets and buzzing flies remind us that we don't have an inalienable right to problem-free existence. They instruct us to take it easy, stop getting uptight, to save our energy for the real challenges of life—big things like cancer and loneliness and death. This is a rather unforeseen benefit of country living!

Where the Sky Springs Free

If the stars should appear
one night in a thousand years,
how would men believe and adore;
and preserve for many generations
the remembrance of the city of God
which has been shown!
But every single night come out
these preachers of beauty,
and light the universe
with their admonishing smile.[10]

Cloud watching could cut spending on therapy in half, and bring down the national debt—an indisputable fact. But since they won't give me a patent on the concept I'll have to keep the secret to myself.

"Honey, I'm going outside to watch clouds," I remarked innocently to Mary Helen as I poured myself a tall glass of iced tea. It was one of those borrowed days in early September short-ly after our move.

"Watch clouds?" she reacted. "What about all those boxes to unpack?"

"At least the grandchildren would understand," I mumbled as I settled down to the serious business of spotting cloud ani-mals. Adjusting the umbrella, I collapsed into one of those tech-nological marvels—a deck chair that didn't leave me with a sore neck and a numb backside. Even though I can be critical of modernity, I'm not a nostalgia nut that has to endure the slatted nightmare that tortured my parents. I sipped my iced tea and gazed around lazily.

Across the road, yellow goldenrod and purple asters framed a field of corn. Two goldfinches chattered from their perch on the TV antenna. Far above, a herd of cows drifted by on a blue pasture. Diaphanous animals meandered across the sky; hippos and giraffes, crocodiles, rhinos, and buffaloes. High streamers of nimbus latticed the blue across which they drifted. Nearer, swal-lows dived and soared and swooped.

When I glanced again at the sky, the scene had changed. The hippo had become an elephant and the crocodile a flock of sheep. A whale swam toward me. And I felt a lot better. In this, Emerson was right:

> *How much tranquillity has been reflected to man from the azure sky, over whose unspotted deeps the winds forevermore drive flocks of stormy clouds, and leave no wrinkle or stain?*[11]

When we moved to the country, we began to rediscover the sky. In the city, a curtain of incandescence had veiled the stars. Neighbouring houses had concealed the advent and egress of the sun. Towers hid the womb where clouds incubate. Smog besmirched the blue of day and smeared the indigo of night. In the city, asphalt and steel, glass and neon brand land and sky with the scars of mankind's sovereignty. Out in the country the sky springs free. Vast. Bold. Alive. It is unsullied by social enigmas, unhurried by the urgency of men and women, unimpressed by the artifacts of another century of arrogance. The sky proclaims transcendence while it spreads a counterpane upon which human dilemmas shrink to their rightful, Lilliputian proportions. No problem is impossible. Hope rides the wildest storm.

As I sipped iced tea, I thought back over the steps that led us here. I remembered how we had scanned the "Out of Town Properties" section in the paper with increasing desperation. Business cards of real estate agents from 100 miles around papered the edges of our bedroom mirror. Property profiles, township maps, and real estate papers cluttered our dining room table. Every weekend, we raided the real estate boxes for the next issue of their dream trust.

Not that we were picky, but since our house was not selling, why not gild our dreams a bit? We decided that our ideal home must be outside a town or village in a country setting within an hour's drive of Toronto. It should have an acre or so of mixed lawn and trees, at least three bedrooms and a garage. We didn't want another renovator's nightmare or high taxes. "And God," we prayed, "if possible, may it be a log house with an open concept and lots of indoor woodwork—and, oh yes, please may it be reasonable enough so that we have some money left over. Amen."

There before me in the intricate dovetail corners of the log wall stood the solid answer to our prayers. How mysterious had been the providence that brought us to this point. How strange that an American from the south and a Canadian from the city should become Northumberland soulmates.

I grew up on the fringe of Toronto before suburbs consumed the fields. Those were the days when Toronto was so dull that little real crime took place. Obviously not a world-class city! My friends and I fished in the creek with bent pins and chased golf balls on what has now become an exclusive golf course. We searched for flares along the railway tracks. We swung on grape vines anchored high in towering oaks in the woods fringing the creek valley. We skinny-dipped at a bend in the Etobicoke Creek where thousands of commuters now nest in towering high rises. We played highway patrol on our bikes along streets now clogged with cars.

After high school, I studied forestry. Summers I canoed, tallied trees, and conducted experiments for various employers. Ever since then, the scent of an old-growth woodlot affects me more than Chanel No. 5. The whisper of wind-blown pines exhilarates me more than the scream of a Corvette on the open road.

Mary Helen grew up in South Carolina cotton country, where girls went barefoot in the summer. She learned to drive a tractor and thump a watermelon. Her dad made homemade sausage and her mom baked "can-I-have-another-piece" cakes that were devoured before they cooled. That was before she became a sophisticated nurse with come-hither brown eyes which melted my heart at a single glance.

We met while I was taking graduate studies in Dixie. Following graduation, we spent sixteen years as missionaries in Pakistan where I concentrated on teaching and writing. When the oldest of our three children graduated from high school, we returned to Toronto to take up a city pastorate. Nine years later, a yearning to find a country setting where I could concentrate more on writing precipitated our common quest.

Ten months into our search, we discovered the Northumberland Hills—an enchanting swath of hilly woodland, farms, and streams east of Toronto. It felt, at last, like home—to both of us. And we quickly fell in love with the country sky that springs so vast and free above the fields and forests.

Seeing that my glass was empty, I wandered inside for a refill. Spotting my soulmate, I persuaded her to join me for some serious therapy—cloud watching. As the afternoon advanced, the horizon became a range of volcanoes spewing flumes of cumulus. The rising wind pushed a herd of trumpeting mastodons before it until only a few patches of blue pasture remained untrampled. Their rumble echoed from the hills. The flashes of their tusks lit up the graying fields. We soon fled inside to watch their charge across the landscape from the picture window. Rain drummed on the roof, then stilled, then dominated the score once more before ceasing abruptly. As the herd thundered east, the luminescence cast up by their hooves coalesced into a shimmering rainbow.

Evening descended and the first star appeared in a sky swept clean by the storm. We have often paused at the front door to gaze up at the night sky, reluctant to go inside after a journey away. The memory of our young daughter, Debbie, asking us one night, "Are there no stars in Canada?" keeps us from taking them for granted.

The question arose after our return from a tour in Asia some years ago. Like many others there, we often slept under the stars during the hot season. We would move our string beds up to the flat roof of our house to catch the evening breeze blowing off the desert. We felt like royalty selecting diamonds and sapphires for a coronation robe as we lay gazing at the shimmer of stars against the black velvet of the night. I'd point out to our three children the Big Dipper, the Milky Way, Orion—exhausting my knowledge, but impressing them. "Daddy, you know everything."

Astronomers, of course, know much, much more: planets and comets, black holes and meteorites, light years and galaxies. Their telescopes push back the frontiers of the universe, as they probe immensity in an attempt to encompass infinity itself. However, each new discovery serves but to uncover some new portal of eternity.

As Whitman perceived, the awesome immensity of the heavens calls us to contemplation more than measurement.

When I heard the learn'd astronomer,
When the proofs, the figures, were ranged in columns before me,
When I was shown the charts and diagrams,
to add, divide and measure them,
When I sitting heard the astronomer where he lectured with
much applause in the lecture-room.
How soon unaccountable I became tired and sick,
Till rising and gliding out I wander'd off by myself,
In the mystical moist night air, and from time to time,
Look'd up in perfect silence at the stars.[12]

Stars—how carelessly we gloss over their mysterious order and immensity. We live and walk and shop and work and love and die beneath their lustre as if they had no message to herald. We take them for granted when they should leave us breathless with praise. A contemporary has paraphrased the ancient bard;

God's glory is on tour in the skies,
God-craft on exhibit across the horizon.
Madame Day holds classes every morning,
Professor Night lectures each evening.

Their words aren't heard,
their voices aren't recorded,
But their silence fills the earth:
unspoken truth is spoken everywhere.

God makes a huge dome
for the sun—a superdome!

The morning sun's a new husband
leaping from his honeymoon bed,
The daybreaking sun an athlete
racing to the tape.

That's how God's Word vaults across the skies
from sunrise to sunset,
Melting ice, scorching deserts,
warming hearts to faith.[13]

Duke's Decision

*Better is a neighbour that is near
than a brother far off.*[14]

With supper in the oven, Mary Helen shouted up the stairs, "Got time for a walk?" I abandoned the computer and replied, "Sure, let's go." One of the great pleasures of country living is being able to walk out the front door and meander down a lane beneath the open sky.

As soon as we closed the door, Duke came bounding down the road to join us. Some burrs clung to his fur where an inky patch joined the tan of his shaggy coat. Duke is the neighbour's dog, a collie, who elected to be our guardian. We met him a couple of days after moving in when we again took up our habit of walking.

That first time, when we crested the rise above our house, he came running toward us loudly protesting our right to walk on his road. Since his pointed nose barely reached our knees, we had to smile at his bravado. His legs were planted a little apart as he fixed his brown eyes on us and tried to look fierce. We thought, "Oh, no. Our dreams of quiet country walks are going to be shattered by hounds."

I had crouched down and held out my hand to pet him. "It's OK fella. We're your new neighbours," I explained. Indifferent, he turned and trotted home, content that he had delivered his warning.

The next time we set out on a walk, Duke trotted out to the road to look us over. He didn't bark this time. And when we called him by name, his tail displayed a flicker of acceptance. Then and there he decided to adopt us. "Obviously," he thought, "these neophytes need an old hand to keep them from getting into trouble." Since that day, whenever we went for a walk, Duke met us at the road with a welcoming twinkle in his brown eyes and a restrained wag of his tail. Then he took us on a tour of his territory.

Author and Duke on Trespass Road

He first led us past the bungalow of his master, our nearest neighbour to the north. Boats and a dozen vehicles lined one side of their property. Half of them looked like rejects from a demolition derby. (Later, when we came to appreciate Randy and his brother Doug's mechanical skill, I learned the truth of that assessment.) Beside the wrecks, the open door of a Quonset hut arced fluorescently where the two brothers worked over a pickup.

When Randy and his wife Kathi first introduced themselves—and Duke—we learned that they, too, were country converts who had moved from town to raise their young family in a rural community. Meeting them proved propitious. That first winter, when an ice storm stranded us halfway up the hill on Trespass Road, it was Randy who towed us behind his truck. Country living, we quickly learned, depends on having good neighbours.

Duke trotted ahead beneath the avenue of black walnuts, past the sandy cut where the bank swallows had their condos, between the wild raspberry bushes to the next neighbour's mailbox where he left his scent.

Duke's nose took him on a zigzag course down the road to Devin and Natalie's long driveway. There, a chipmunk led him on a merry chase along their fence row. Spooked, Natalie's three horses galloped across the pasture. Devin and Natalie embody neighbourliness. Both of them wave at us from their truck whenever they see us outside in our garden. If Natalie passes us when we are out on a walk, she often stops to chat. That first winter when we were snowed in, she brought us milk and eggs in her 4 x 4. In the spring, Devin shared some of his fresh asparagus. Although we never came to know them well, we realized that here was a couple who would respond to any emergency we might have.

Beyond their Victorian reproduction, the road narrowed where Duke led us through a stretch of woods. Isolated from dwellings, this patch is our cathedral. The branches of maples and oaks arch over the road, creating a sanctuary. At either end white pines soar heavenward like gothic towers. In the rustle of leaves and the trill of songbirds, "All nature sings and round us rings the music of the spheres."

The vestments of each season present a parade of loveliness unrivaled by mediaeval craftsmen. Summer weaves hangings of rich emerald brocade. Fall casts a carpet of scarlet and gold beneath our feet. Winter drapes the cloister in wool. Spring crochets a filigree of brown and lemon green.

Like an usher, Duke escorted us through the vestibule, past the copse where we first saw the red fox, beyond the intersection of the snowmobile trail, to the hillock where a thicket of lilac hid the ruins of a pioneer homestead. Refusing to go further, his brown eyes pleaded with us to turn around. In the swale below, a German shepherd, whose territory Duke will not challenge, patrolled a farmyard.

Yielding to Duke's entreaty, we turned back. Suddenly, Duke stopped, tilted his head and turned to stare behind us. An old truck appeared on the crest of a distant hill coming our way. Minutes dragged by as we continued our stroll before we stepped off the road to make way for the approach of a battered Ford pickup. Some trucks fly by, scattering gravel. This truck was going so slow it seemed to be stuck in first gear.

As it rattled by, I had time to study the two occupants. (Much later we learned their names.) Clarence, the driver, turned his weathered face toward me with a barely perceptible nod. He wore an old feed cap and a faded plaid shirt. His eyes seemed haunted by some inner pain. His wife Mae stared straight ahead. Her pinched face was gaunt and lined, her eyes dark and small, like two black raisins, her white hair done up in a severe bun. She wore a Mother Hubbard dress of an indeterminate shade of blue with a pattern of barely discernable flowers.

We stared after them with ill-concealed curiosity. Their faces reflected a lifetime of toil. Or was it tragedy? Did they reminisce about children in far off foreign lands? Or grieve for land lost to the bank? Did they once live along Trespass Road?

Duke bounded ahead of us after the retreating pickup. On this day, as always, Duke left us where his driveway met the lane leading to the Zikowski farm. As we went by, we waved at Lev Zikowski who was checking the electric fence after moving his cattle into the pasture along the road. When we got snowed in that first winter, Lev cleared our driveway, and if he's not careful with that fence, his cattle would feast on our flowers.

Our neighbour to the south was cutting his grass while his wife weeded their flower beds. Since we see them rarely, we ambled over to ask how things were going. Although Daphne works in the city two or three days a week and Robin keeps close to his computer, they have become our most dependable neighbours. When they are away on a trip, we keep an eye on their house and check for mail. They do the same for us. When I punched a hole in the wall while doing what I thought were repairs, Robin had a patch of drywall to cover the hole. Although we are not back-fence type neighbours, we know that we can call on each other in an emergency.

Country neighbours are a lot like Duke: suspicious at first, even a bit aloof, slow to warm up, independent, careful to guard their privacy. But they are dependable, available when the need arises. They follow Herbert's advice, "Love your neighbour, yet pull not down your hedge."[15]

Of course, some neighbours make an art of privacy. Six years later we still didn't know who lived down the lane at the dip in the hill. Perhaps the credo of some coincides with that of Emily Murphy in "Janey Canuck;"

The greatest pleasure of country life
is in having no neighbours.

Why should I tolerate neighbours
when I cannot tolerate myself?[16]

In the country there is even room for that opinion. Fortunately, it is not held by many. Out here, people need each other. When an aged recluse down at the crossroads found himself evicted and his house condemned, people pitched in to bring his house up to code. When a house burned down ten miles away, everyone emptied their pockets to offer some cash. Of course the fire department is staffed by volunteers. We sure need them!

People out here know your name. The librarian not only knows my name but my library card number! And when I went to the polling booth to vote in a recent township election, I discovered that the registrar was the mother of the boy who helped me stack wood. Even though there is not much anonymity here—the country grapevine is omniscient—it's kind of nice to know you are not just a street number. The sign down at the corner gas station is symbolic. It announces more engagements, births and anniversaries than it advertises chips, pop and videos.

Since that day, however, when he decided to adopt us, Duke has remained our most devoted neighbour. His faithfulness over the years astounds us. Whatever the weather, whatever the time of day, Duke races to join us in our walks. In drizzle he shakes off the drops dripping from his black nose and guides us around the puddles. In snow he plunges through the drifts searching for field mice. Even when the heat of summer sends him searching for shade, the sound of our footsteps on the road brings him running to our side. When he fails to appear, we worry.

To think we almost didn't find this place! Ten months into our search, exhaustion dogged our steps. Occasionally we drove by the log house on Trespass Road, but the asking price extinguished the flicker of interest that kept rising from the ashes of frustration. We determined not to fall in love with the place.

However, Bob, our local real estate agent, kept rekindling our hopes. The owners had bought another house and were impatient to move east. Their asking price continued to fall. In spite of our reticence, Bob urged us to visit the site and make an offer—whatever we could afford.

Reluctantly, we examined our budget and made an offer—then we held our breath, watched the phone, and prayed a lot. After negotiating a small increase, the owners accepted! Euphoria reigned.

A month later, we unlocked the door on a new chapter in our lives. We remember wandering through the house hand-in-hand. In the living room, we surveyed the warm log walls with wonder and did a little jig. We tiptoed over the pine floors upstairs to peek into each room. We opened cupboard doors. We tried the taps and flushed the toilet. We peered through the skylights at the gathering dusk.

Eight years on, we still remark about the gentle providence that led us down this country byway. In spite of invading crickets, mice in the attic, and skunks on the lawn, we continue to regale friends about our country adventure. For we have good neighbours, an expansive sky, and yes, we were adopted by a border collie named Duke.

Neighbours, we have found, take on an importance in the country that they don't have in the cities. You can live for years in an apartment in London or New York and barely speak to the people who live six inches away from you on the other side of a wall. In the country, separated from the next house though you may be by hundreds of yards, your neighbours are part of your life, and you are part of theirs.[17]

Hallelujah Hill

The grace that is a tree
belongs to me;
the quietness of stone
I make my own;
From the strong hills I borrow.
My flesh itself is kin
to earth and all therein
and of my brother's heart
I am a part.[18]

Computers and faxes enable us to do most of our work at home. However, we do have to travel to the city quite frequently. When we do, urban re-entry frazzles our nerves and frustration dogs our commute home. Sometimes we even question our flight into the country—just a little.

I vividly recall one warm day last September. We were drunk from a diesel-fume-cocktail, frightened by towering transports, and stalled in a traffic snarl on what comics call a "freeway." We had not moved for twenty minutes.

We rolled up the window to shut out the fumes. But before we did, we caught snatches of country music from the nearest semi. "I was country when country wasn't cool," crooned the singer.

"Cool? Ha! You have to be crazy to be country," I grumbled. "Right about now, I can see the wisdom of owning a condo downtown."

"We only face this torture once in awhile," Mary Helen responded. "What about people who run the gauntlet every day?"

"Maybe we're all crazy," I fumed as the minutes dragged by.

Fortunately, it's not very often that we get caught up in this maelstrom. As soon as we could, we took an exit and turned north ten miles to the Ganaraska Road. Heading east, the rolling hills quickly restored our perspective. How? Reasons people like us choose country living were spread out all along this roller coaster highway.

The first hill we breasted was banded by orange ski lifts like an adolescent smile imprisoned by braces. We coasted down past "Honey for sale" on the left, "Twig furniture for sale" on the right and the Quinton House Bed & Breakfast on the left. On the banks of the Ganaraska, they host mystery weekends and serve proper "English Cream Teas" on the lawn. Up and down its length, the Ganaraska Road celebrates the independence and entrepreneurship of fascinating people.

We entered Northumberland County in a long "S" curve that climbs past a collapsed barn on one side and a thriving dairy operation on the other. Topping a long rise, we raced down another hill into Elizabethville (pop. 25) with its archetypical stream, pond, tiny church, and the "60 kph" speed limit signs that are impossible to obey without standing on the brakes. Beaver Meadow Road veers off to the left.

Snaking cedar swamps inhabited by deer and beaver line this gravel spur before it climbs out of the valley to end at a picture-perfect stud farm where some of Ontario's best horseflesh is bred. In the country there's space—lots of space—to exercise shank's mare or ride a pinto, hunt or birdwatch, ski cross country or race snowmobiles on ice, fish, or just watch the clouds drift by.

Temptation crests the next rise, introduced in advance by the silhouette of a pioneer woman advertising, "Betty's Pies & Tarts." The attached garage of a brick bungalow converted into a bake shop flaunts the indomitable spirit of country entrepreneurship. It looks like another doomed attempt to wrest a living from marginal land. How could a woman hope to sell tarts in the middle of nowhere? Taste! Her butter tarts, sausage rolls, and blueberry pies draw customers from all over.

From "Betty's" I had hardly shifted into third before the hallelujahs began to rise unbidden from deep within. We crested Dean's Hill to rediscover our valley spread out below. No one but us knows that we have baptized it "Hallelujah Hill." We felt an injection of energy as the car picked up speed to race down the slope like a stallion scenting a filly. We had seen the country sampler spread out in the valley below many times but once again, the weariness of travel evaporated.

The horizon on the north is framed by the sylvan hills of the Ganaraska Forest. On the south, patchwork farms march to the horizon. Like a tailor's shears, the highway slices through a quilt stitched by rows of zigzag cedars. These cedar seams separate patches of hardwood bush, pastures dotted with grazing cattle, and fields of ripening corn. Here and there houses and barns, like toys on a childhood counterpane, peek out from under gnarled maples and wind-blown pine. Nestled in the middle of this calico quilt, a village church raises its spire heavenward.

Why do people love the country? The scenery. The scent of cedar on the breeze. The sight of a six-point buck. Fresh air. A storm rattling the windows. Space. The seasons. The beauty. Yes, beauty that breaks through the hard crust of a heart chained by daytimers and balance sheets.

Our descent down Hallelujah Hill took us past a squat school that must have been designed by a drunken architect during one of those periods when utility triumphed over beauty. Five ugly portables aggravated the image. Not everything in the country is pretty. We passed the red brick United Church—established in 1880—to turn north over the creek at the gas station with its dozens of rusting cars and its sign announcing; "Happy Anniversary Harv & Bev." The gas station also serves as the post office.

If we had been shopping in Port Hope we would have approached this corner from Turkey Hill, the handful of houses that locals call "Perrytown." Ever since that cold January when I saw the flock of wild turkeys scratching in the soybean fields below the pioneer cemetery, it has been Turkey Hill to me. That winter, they ventured as far as our road, but since then, hunters seem to have flushed them deep into the cedar stands along the Ganaraska.

On the opposite side of our valley from Turkey Hill, a dense stand of evergreens crowns the top of another headland, except for a clear-cut pasture on its eastern slope. In the middle of that pasture, like a knob on a knee, stands a clump of pine. An artist living near Turkey Hill pointed it out to us. In her mind, it was Pimple Hill. Our home nestles on the lee of a highland just beyond that pimple of pine. When the grandchildren were with me one day, I christened it Cupcake Hill. Much better to say we live just beyond Cupcake Hill than Pimple Hill. Our granddaughters love Grandma's cupcakes.

Within view of our three hills—Hallelujah Hill, Turkey Hill, and Cupcake Hill—people do the usual things that people do in any rural community. We have beef farmers, real estate agents, and mechanics, electricians, and market gardeners. People rent videos, play the lottery, and sometimes go to church. They cheer the local baseball teams and make love. Many demonstrate a startling degree of individuality. In the valley, a water-driven mill still grinds flour. One woman raises goats while another grows wild flowers for sale. One farm sells garlic and glads. Another farms trout. In the shelter of the forested hills, the McConnell's raise pheasants. Keith teaches people to fly ultralights. Several men race stock cars. A craftsman assembles log homes.

Why do people live in the country? In the country, people find freedom to experiment with their dreams without being totally stifled by bylaws. There is room to imagine what might be; there is space to soar.

Near home, we passed a tiny log cabin nestled in the cedars. A battered racing car rested in the shade. Turning off the highway, we climbed up Trespass Road under over-arching pines, passed a hayfield, and turned down our gravel drive.

Home again. The release of that smoggy weariness garnered from a day in the "big smoky" produced a country high that beats Jack Daniel's any day. Why do I love thee? Let me count the ways....

FALL

Cattlemen Prefer Blondes

All things with which we deal, preach to us.
What is a farm but a mute gospel?
The chaff and the wheat, weeds and plants,
blight, rain, insects, sun,
—it is a sacred symbol
from the first furrow of spring
to the last stack
which the snow of winter
overtakes in the fields.[19]

October was beginning to whisper "be gone" to September. I stood on the deck sipping a cup of tea while I savoured the first blush of autumn's palette on the maples. Lev was rumbling across the hayfield to the west. He was working to bale a late cutting before another storm broke. The 400-pound bales multiplied around the field like the pieces in a giant's crokinole game. Eyeing their precarious positions on the slope, I imagined one of them rolling into our living room.

Since age six, when a country cousin threatened to serve up my fox terrier as a hot dog, I've stood in mortal awe of farmers. Lev epitomizes that hardy race. He works alone. His two brothers took nine-to-five jobs in the city. His sister is a school teacher in another county. Arthritis keeps his father indoors. No matter, he runs cattle on two farms, one near us, and another on a distant concession.

In the evening when we go out for a walk, he often passes us coming from, or going to, his second farm. It's not that Lev races from job to job. He works slowly, methodically, like a perpetual-motion machine: cutting hay; planting winter wheat; combining soybeans; harvesting corn for winter silage; stringing electric fence; moving cattle from pasture to pasture; cleaning stables; storing hay; spreading manure; ploughing; disking; seeding; cultivating. Through all the seasons, without a break, he never stops.

His pickup sports a rebel flag in the back window and a bumper sticker announcing, "Cattlemen prefer blondes." The Dixie flag signifies a farmer's independence. The bumper sticker—far more than a breed of cattle—I'm sure symbolizes an impossible desire. You see, Lev is married to his tractor.

When I first met him sipping coffee at the country store, I didn't have the nerve to inquire. A cap advertising, Co-op, shaded Lev's gunmetal eyes and boxer's nose. Exposure had stained his face the colour of strong tea and fissured his lean good looks. Although his mouth betrayed a dour sense of humour, his corded arms and work-thickened hands warned of brute strength. He wore mechanic's coveralls and boots bearing the scars of half a decade's toil.

Remarkably, our history is linked to one of our farm neighbours. A title search reveals that our property is a severance from land cleared by pioneers named Wright whose descendants still populate this township. A neighbouring farm, in turn, is a purchase from their progeny. If we scratch deep enough in the dust that has settled over our past, most of us will discover a farm heritage.

Although our connection to this land and this particular farmer is tenuous, our dependence on a farm heritage is certain. Mary Helen's ancestors tamed the wild red soil of South Carolina. Her grandfather was cheated out of his share of a plantation. My maternal forebears parlayed their status as shepherds and drovers in Scotland into a prosperous farm in Ontario. A generation later, the elder brother put his siblings through college while he stayed on the farm. Two became renowned engineers, one going on to become the president of Cornell. Two became doctors, one of whom distinguished herself among Ontario's first lady doctors. One became a high-school teacher. Our family is not unusual. Most people have farmers perched somewhere in their family tree.

The stump fences and stone piles that line sections of our

country road offer mute testimony to the struggles of the pioneers: overgrown, ignored, forgotten, sinking into the soil. These are not the relics of war. They do not echo with the sound of ghost-cannon nor hide the bones of the slain. More likely they bear sweat-soaked fingerprints; they echo to the sound of axe and the grunt of oxen. Along with the land that sweeps in a green billow from fence row to forest glade, they are the monuments of our pioneers. They enshrine the real history of our land.

In an attempt to understand some of the history buried in the soil where we live, I dug around a bit. I discovered that for generations a Mississauga village, named Cochingomink, had stood at the mouth of the Ganaraska River. From that base they had fished for giant sturgeon in Lake Ontario and hunted the forests all the way to Rice Lake. In 1778, Peter Smith, "the fairest and best liked of all the men trading along the lake," established a trading post at Cochingomink. In 1793, a few pioneers began to clear land in allotments laid out in Hope Township. They prosaically renamed Cochingomink, Smith Creek. The building of a grist mill and a saw mill on the river in 1795 encouraged a further influx of settlers. By 1803, the population of the Hope Township had swelled to 277. Smith Creek became Port Hope.[20]

Every county in every country has a history rooted in the soil. There is something about working with the soil that produces character—patience, perseverance, determination, honest labour, rugged individualism, community loyalty, ingenuity.

Not all farm products are as wholesome as these. Take guilt for instance. While guilt doesn't only grow in country soil, nothing can send you on a guilt trip faster than watching a farmer at work. A cousin, who fled his farm heritage to pursue a career in education, explained it to me one day.

"My father worked from sunup to after sunset. His days were measured by yards of fence erected, acres of sod ploughed, numbers of cows milked, loads of manure spread, bushels of wheat sown. Value was calibrated in bales of hay, bushels of wheat, and pounds of milk. Your worth depended on what you did and what you produced. From early morning to late at night, you were expected to fill up the time with measurable chores that might earn you the respite of sleep. No time for frivolity. No time for reading, except perhaps an agricultural journal. No time for flights of imagination.

"I inhaled this ethic with every furrow I ploughed. My father taught me that the farmer is a co-worker with God—part of the great scheme of things. Factory workers and their white-collar cousins who push paper, well, they waste their lives. What comes from the land is special. When asthma gave me an excuse to flee the farm, I took it. But even though years have gone by, the black dog of guilt has been pursuing me ever since. I have to keep reminding myself that the labour of a teacher, the work of a musician, the ideas of a writer are just as valuable as the ploughing of a farmer."

This hound from hell pursues all of us. He devalues the implements of the mind, the imagination, and the heart. He scorns rest and reflection as indolence. He whispers that our value depends on what we can produce, whether that be dollars or widgets or bushels of wheat. We can still his accusations only by activity—work, projects, busyness.

In its farm incarnation, this exaggerated work ethic provokes classic disagreement. Thoreau caricatured farmers as serfs, bound to the soil.

I see young men... serfs of the soil...
crushed and smothered under a load,
creeping down the road of life,
pushing before [them] a barn seventy-five feet by forty,

its Augean stables never cleansed
and one hundred acres of land, tillage, mowing, pasture, and
wood-lot![21]

His friend Emerson, on the other hand, saw the farm as a gospel full of sacred symbolism. Clearly, we need some balance here! Rest and recreation to balance unstinting labour. As someone has said, "Farming is one of the finest occupations in the world if taken in moderation."[22]

We probably can't do much to inject balance into a profession where many are fighting to stave off bankruptcy. But why not celebrate our farming heritage? Quite wisely, we remember our soldiers with poppies and a moment of silence on November eleventh. We could remember our farm heritage as well by declaring some Saturday in winter, when farmers have the least to do, Farm Heritage Day. Everyone could wear a sprig of wheat!

Lev had finished haying and moved on to his field of soybeans. With one eye on an approaching storm, he gauged their readiness for harvest.

Go to the ant, you sluggard; consider its ways and be wise! It has no commander, no overseer or ruler, Yet it stores its provisions in summer, and gathers its food at harvest. How long will you lie there, you sluggard? When will you get up from your sleep? A little sleep, a little slumber, a little folding of the hands to rest—and poverty will come on you like a bandit and scarcity like an armed man.[23]

In vain you rise early and stay up late,
toiling for food to eat—for he grants sleep to those he loves.[24]

Country Carousel

Here, as I sit—the sunlight on my face,
And shadows of green leaves upon mine eyes—
My heart, a garden in a hidden place,
Is full of folded buds of memories.[25]

G randchildren give you a second kick at the can without the pain of stubbing your toe. Or, as Solomon commented, "children's children are a crown" to the mature.[26] One fall we had a chance to relive childhood.

"Hi grandpa! Hi grandma!" waved three-year-old Kassandra through a watermelon grin as she floated past on a painted horse. We were at the Roseneath Fall Fair, watching our grandchildren ride a carousel. A few years earlier, the need for costly repairs had silenced its magical sound forever—so it seemed. Now it has been beautifully restored. Why would a tiny village go to such lengths to refurbish a relic?

Roseneath is a country crossroads with the usual scattering of houses. It boasts a general store, a tiny restaurant, a combined pizza parlour and convenience store, a craft shop, a couple of churches, a consolidated school and very little else—except the fairgrounds. They dominate the village.

We threaded our way through a confusion of dusty trucks, shiny vans, cars and 4 x 4's. Cars pinched Highway 45 into an hourglass through the village. They overran driveways onto lawns. They blanketed the school grounds. We finally found a spot on a slope behind the school and paid a few bucks to enter the fair. Inexpensive!

Sleepy Roseneath rocked. The bawl of loudspeakers from the country music hoe-down fought a losing battle with the blare of amplifiers from the midway. During the occasional lull in this combat, a few bars of hurdy-gurdy music from the carousel pierced the dust rising above the scene. The cacophony drowned out the couple singing gospel on the football field. The only ones who heard their sweet sound were those examining the ring of antique cars nearby.

In the centre of the fairgrounds stands the jewel of Rose-neath, a carousel crafted in Abilene, Kansas in 1906. It was there that we had arranged to meet our daughter Debbie, her husband Brian, and their three girls.

After hugs all around, we joined the lineup for tickets. An amazing cross-section of society rode the brightly lacquered horses. Seniors drifted by in a cloud of nostalgia. Children waved to parents and smiled at each other. A young mother crooned to her newborn child. Teens had left their sometimes prickly self-consciousness behind. The rise and descent of the horses, the slow circuit beneath the painted tin roof, the steady beat of the music cast a spell. Worries and quarrels piled up outside the entrance. The mood was mellow. No wonder more adults than children climbed on-board this sentimental journey.

When our turn came, sedate seven-year-old Shareena chose a white steed with red trim. Five-year-old Adrianna, our blonde mischief, picked a black stallion. Kassandra, a brown-haired pixie, chose one decorated in gold and blue. Brian and Debbie stood beside them as they glided up and down to a sound as old as childhood itself.

Kassandra, Debbie, Shareena, Adrianna and Brian on the carousel.

After promising another ride, we headed for the show barn. To one side as perfect a row of sheep as I had ever seen were being judged. With their black heads, ivory-snow bodies, and black stockings they looked like ladies-in-waiting being inspected before the arrival of a queen. Inside we took our place along the railing of the arena. "The cows are so white—so clean!" exclaimed Shareena as she pointed to Holsteins being led around the ring by teenagers in 4H jerseys. Clean cows! Combed sheep! Shareena perceived a trend. The farm animals she had known were always smelly and splattered with mud.

From the judging ring, we passed into Chicken Little Land. Hens and roosters of every imaginable size and colour strutted their stuff. "Daddy, that rooster looks like the rainbow," exclaimed Adrianna. "How come there are so many different kinds of chickens? I thought there was just one kind. Huh, daddy?"

"I don't know honey," her dad replied, "I guess God likes variety."

"Pigs!" squealed Kassandra sidling up carefully to a dozen little piglets suckling a prize sow. "Look at the rabbits over here," called Shareena from another corner while Adrianna begged us to let her feed the draft horse in the corner. There were row upon row of stalls full of combed and curried, scrubbed and sanitized calves and horses, sheep and goats, donkeys and turkeys, pheasants and chickens.

"Don't get too close to those geese," cautioned their mother.

"We never got this close to animals in the zoo," remarked Shareena as she tried to decide whether to pet the rabbits or feed the horse.

Outside the show barn, the midway beckoned. Victims on the revolving ferris wheel squealed as it rocked to a stop, leaving them swinging high in the air. Prey locked in the Hurricane shrieked. Teens on bumper cars crashed each other with wild abandon to the accompaniment of an electric buzz. Row upon row of teaser booths beckoned. "A winner every time" proclaimed the ball throw, the dart game and the fishing pond. "Can we win a prize daddy, can we, please?" wheedled all three of the girls together.

After we had expressed suitable appreciation for the junk they won, Adrianna put on her most serious face to explain, "I really like cotton candy, Grandpa."

"So do I sweetheart," I replied, heading toward the sign

marked, "Candy Apples - Cotton Candy."

"And french fries," the other two exclaimed.

Dogs. Burgers. Fries. Sausage on a bun. Fairs create lots of hungry people. Forget about cholesterol for a day. So while Mary Helen cleaned up the ketchup and mustard splattered on a picnic table, Brian and I went foraging.

After sharing cotton candy and fries, Brian took the kids to buy balloons twisted into animal shapes. Mary Helen and I became fascinated by a taffy-making operation. The longest line-up at the fair snaked down the midway in front of this booth manned by three generations from one family. Behind the trailer, Grandpa stirred a black pot of candy over a propane burner. Beside him one son cooled another pot in a water barrel. Another worked rhythmically with a dark skein of taffy out front. He alternately threw it over a hook on the trailer, stretched it almost to breaking point and doubled it up over the hook, only to stretch it out again. Before our eyes the skein gradually lightened in colour until he judged it ready for cutting.

When he plopped it down on a long table, three generations were waiting to cut and wrap each piece. "That makes thirty lots already," one commented to the matriarch. Her recipe had proven so popular that the whole family spent their weekends going from fair to fair. People in the know bought half-a-dozen bags to take home.

We continued to wander. There were sulkies to watch, antique cars to inspect, gospel music to enjoy, halls full of exhibits to examine, the start of a house built out of bales of straw to ponder, square dancers to mark time with. Finally, as the golden afternoon waned, we caught up with the family at the carousel.

Shareena chose a red stallion this time while Adrianna opted for brown palouse. Kassandra waved from her perch on a grinning golden steed. The Wurlitzer Player organ struck up its signature

tune. The lilting melody, part hurdy-gurdy, part circus, catapult-
ed me back—back to a childhood buried beneath the debris of
years, beyond sadness, beyond disappointments, before I erected
the prim structure of grown-up responsibility. Memories of childhood innocence surfaced, but so indistinct I couldn't trace
them—chimeras from the fantasy world where children dream.

Adrianna on the carousel.

No wonder Roseneath cherishes its treasure. The golden age
of carousel construction ended with the Great Depression.
Those remaining from that earlier era are locked away in private
collections or glorified in public displays. This particular
carousel, with its forty wooden horses and two boats, left the
C.W. Parker plant in Abilene, Kansas in 1906. Then it dropped
from sight. Eventually it surfaced in Brantford, Ontario. In
1932, the Roseneath Agricultural Fair Board purchased it as the
centrepiece for their fair.

By 1986, Ontario safety standards and soaring insurance
costs seemed to doom the fair's tiara. Should they sell it to eager
American collectors or to Ottawa's Museum of Man? Or should

they declare the carousel of historic value and restore its splendour to meet heritage criteria? The cost? $400,000—far beyond the means of a tiny village.

Nevertheless, the community was determined to save their jewel and expand its use beyond the week of the fall fair. A tiny group of volunteers organized a restoration committee. They conceived the idea of putting the horses up for adoption at $5,000 apiece. Friends nation-wide helped to fund the project. With funds in hand, they were able to bring artist-cum-sculptor Konstantin Walberg from Germany to painstakingly restore the steeds to their former lustre. Now that the restoration is complete on the carousel, the merry sound of its music can be heard throughout the summer.

Life consists not only in today's activities and tomorrow's plans. Yesterday's happy memories flower long after they are picked. We would do well to sow prodigiously, that we might have armfuls of blooms to brighten the gloomiest corners of our mental archives.

It was Mary Helen who marked indelibly the expedition to the Roseneath fair on our calendar. She has the marvelous facility of setting the stage for happy memories. Nowadays, she is busy creating memories in the minds of our grandchildren. In yesteryear, she crammed our own children's minds with mementos to carry through life—birthday parties, picnics, shopping junkets, Thanksgiving, Christmas, Easter. If she found no reason to celebrate, she created a reason.

I tried, not always successfully, to sublimate my own Scroogy annoyance at being interrupted from "important work" to help her. I did help plan expeditions to the desert, the seashore, and the mountains. Travels home from Asia enabled us to visit the British parliament and the Colosseum in Rome, the Parthenon in Athens and temples in Kyoto. However, Mary Helen has remained the ultimate memory-maker. In retrospect, I honour her calling more than I did at the time. Blessed are they who create happy memories!

> *Oft in the stilly night,*
> *Ere Slumber's chain has bound me,*
> *Fond Memory brings the light*
> *Of other days around me;*
> *The smile, the tears,*
> *Of boyhood years,*
> *The words of love then spoken;*
> *The eyes that shone*
> *Now dimmed and gone,*
> *The cheerful hearts now broken.*[27]

Judging sheep at Roseneath Fall Fair.

A Sumac Thanksgiving

In this shrill moon the scouts of Winter ran
From the ice-belted north, and whistling shafts
Struck maple and struck sumac, and a blaze
Ran swift from leaf to leaf, from bough to bough,
Till round the forest flashed a belt of flame.[28]

Since early morning we'd been preparing the Thanksgiving dinner. Nine would sit down to turkey and all the fixin's. My job was to thaw and stuff the turkey. Wrestling with a frozen bird before my first cup of coffee is murder. I was trying to force it to disgorge its severed neck from the cavity where the diabolical butchers had stuffed it before freezing.

"Why can't they just attach it to a leg by a rubber band," I grumbled to Mary Helen.

In spite of years of honing my technique, I never seem to get the neck and giblets free without a dangerous rise in blood pressure. My most successful Thanksgivings were those when I delegated the job to our son or son-in-law.

"Just be thankful you have a turkey to stuff!" Mary Helen rejoined as she prepared sweet potato soufflé according to a secret southern recipe.

When I finally wrested the neck and giblets from the turkey's cavity, I turned my attention to the stuffing. From scratch: bread, celery, walnuts, margarine, spices. "You can't make too much stuffing," John, our youngest son, had warned.

With the aroma of roasting turkey torturing our taste buds, people began to arrive. The kitchen drew everyone like lodestone. Some wanted to peek into the oven at the turkey. The grandchildren talked all at once, bringing us up-to-date on what had been happening in their lives. No wonder the marshmallow topping on the soufflé burned.

The table was set, the turkey carved. People had found their places. A hush descended. In our family, we have a Thanksgiving tradition that, before grace, each one shares something for which they are thankful.

"I'm thankful for Shona," said our son John as he looked into the eyes of his sweetheart. "And I for John," Shona replied with a smile. Marriage suited them well.

"Thank you Grandma," whispered Kassandra, who was eighteen months at the time. Savouring the occasion to try out a new phrase, she repeated this refrain throughout the day. "You're welcome, Punkin," Mary Helen replied.

"I'm thankful for my family—for Brian, and for God providing Mom and Dad with this wonderful country home!" responded our daughter Debbie.

"Thank you Mummy and Daddy!" interjected Kassandra, gathering momentum. "You're welcome, Sweetheart," smiled Debbie.

Others added their appreciation for friends and family, for the country air, for God's goodness, for the Northumberland Hills, and for the beauty of autumn. Mary Helen was the last to speak.

"I'm thankful that although Steve and Catherine and their family couldn't be with us, they chatted on the phone," she said. She deeply misses Steve, our oldest son, who lives in New Zealand with his wife and three children. "And I'm thankful for sumac," she concluded.

Thankful for sumac? True, its scarlet tints shimmered off the crystal glasses on our thanksgiving table like reflections from a troupe of tribal dancers. Between the platter of turkey, the bowls of succotash and mashed potatoes, the tureen of sweet potato soufflé and all the garnishes, Mary Helen had scattered sumac leaves to decorate the Thanksgiving table.

Why be thankful for this useless bush? Pulpy and stunted, it's no good for firewood. It sends out underground suckers that spoil our lawn. It shades out young conifers and hardwoods. Autumn is its only moment of glory. Why did God make such a useless plant so prolific? It thrives along fence lines and at the edges of woodlots in many parts of North America.

Perhaps "useless" is a label we apply to cover our own ignorance. How many plants and insects of nature do we ignore—or
despise—due to lack of knowledge? Research turns up the information that our native peoples dried an abundance of the sticky
red berries to use in the winter. They taught settlers how to prepare
a refreshing sumac drink and how to avoid the poisonous variety.
Some outdoorsy types mix sumac berries with elderberries.[29]

Suppose, however, no practical use is found. Would that
banish sumac from our Thanksgiving? Surely, beauty itself is to
be valued. Especially that which heralds the passing of the seasons, captures the fading warmth of summer, and foretells the
approach of the golden days. Sumac is among the very first to
feel the blush of autumn's frost. As if a toddler, or perhaps a surrealist, had been let loose with a brush dipped in scarlet, sumac
paints the hills with strokes of colour startling in their boldness.

Giving thanks for what we take for granted... that's a
healthy habit! Thanks for Mary Helen, whose brown eyes cap-
ture beauty in strange places. Thanks for everything we take for
granted: clean water, friends and neighbours, the expansive sky,
hills and valleys, grasses along the roadway, marriage, wild asters
and goldenrod, grandchildren, strength to work. And thanks for
pioneers, who paused in the midst of adversity to give thanks for
the harvest.

Someone has written, "He who forgets the language of
thanksgiving will never be on speaking terms with happiness."
John Henry Jowet comments, "Gratitude is a vaccine, an antitoxin, and an antiseptic." Did he mean a vaccine against
despair, an antitoxin to counter discouragement, an antiseptic
to banish gloom?

Some people have obviously been inoculated against looking
on the bright side. Pessimism colours everything they say and do.
Others, however, seem to bubble over with gratitude for the

smallest mercies. After visiting many seniors in the twilight of
their lives, I have come to a sobering, although not very profound,
conclusion. I remind myself of this conclusion whenever I grump
and groan. Attitudes adopted when we are younger either crater
our pathway with potholes into which we keep stumbling, or
smooth out the eroded track of advancing age. We can either turn
sour and grumpy or learn, with Kassandra, to be thankful.

> *An easy thing, O Power Divine,*
> *To thank Thee for these gifts of Thine,*
> *For summer's sunshine, winter's snow,*
> *For hearts that kindle, thoughts that glow.*
> *But when shall I attain to this—*
> *To thank Thee for the things I miss?*[30]

Where God Rakes Leaves

Along the line of smoky hills
The crimson forest stands,
And all the day the blue-jay calls
Throughout the Autumn lands.[31]

The gnarled old sugar maple by the village church, always the first to turn crimson, was already bare. Apples and potatoes had replaced corn and broccoli at Aikens Country Market. Signs announced, "Potatoes, $10 for 50 lb." "Windfalls, $6 a bushel." Overnight, pumpkins appeared on porches and gateposts. And Jack Frost had stolen Ms. Field's summer dress leaving behind a tan and russet tie-dye.

On our own acre, the sumac was aflame beneath the pines. Our soft maple blushed cherry red. No wonder it is called red maple—not to be confused with its only slightly less dramatic cousin, the sugar (or hard) maple. The annuals drooped in shriveled clumps leaving the flower beds bedraggled, except for the odd cosmos, some late-blooming phlox, and a rose bush with a pink bloom like a peony. "More exquisite than any other is the autumn rose."[32] To many of us, fall is more appealing than any other season.

Life in the fall becomes urgent in northern climes as we store up images for the days ahead. At no time is this more true than during those lazy days of Indian summer when mild weather halts the approach of winter. After a few weeks of frost, the sun again brings blue skies and warm days. Short sleeves banish sweaters to the back of the closet.

In one of her cartoon strips, Lynn Johnston pictures the magic of the season through the eyes of her daughter, April. April skips with the carefree abandon of the very young through autumn leaves. She tosses leaves to her dog, who jumps and leaps to catch them. Discovering how they crunch under her feet, she marches back and forth like a play soldier. Next she collects a great pile, only to scatter them skyward. Her eyes widen as she surveys the rainbow of colours spread around her feet. She stands stock still, awed as one might be in a great cathedral, while she watches leaves drift lazily down from their backyard maple. Suddenly, she hugs herself!

At this point her teenage sister wanders out to ask, "April, what are you doing?" April replies, "Trying to make today last longer."[33]

With the sun of Indian summer glinting off golden hillsides, "trying to make the day last longer" seemed a very sensible thing to do. Its siren song drowned out the shrill voice of my conscience badgering me to finish an assignment, tidy the flower beds, re-caulk the windows, dig the potatoes, pile wood, pay those bills, answer letters… "Honey, let's go for a walk."

Leaving her sewing project, Mary Helen joined me. Scarcely had we shut the door before Duke spied us from his lookout up the hill and trotted down to greet us. With a wave of his tail he led the way towards the fence line where we could gaze over the valley. Sniffing roadside bushes, he left his scent and moved on. We lingered to drink deeply of the coronation below.

Trembling aspen crowned a far hill with a diadem of gold. The light breeze orchestrated their shimmer into a delicate minuet. Patches of green pine, bronze oak, and scarlet maple clothed the hill below the aspen like the robe in a royal pageant. Fingers of hemlock and orderly rows of cedar stitched the robe where it met the spring-fed valley. Each tree had its own signature—a combination of tint and texture so unique that we could pick out the composition of the forest from miles away.

In this, Emerson was right:

> *Such is the constitution of all things... that the primary forms, as the sky, the mountain, the tree, the animal, give us a delight in and for themselves; a pleasure arising from outline, color, motion, and grouping.*[34]

As we leaned against the old fence, tendrils of pure pleasure linked us together in silent homage to the divine Artist who crowned the harvest season with such rich abandon.

Duke looked at us impatiently, willing us to move along. Sighing with contentment, we turned back. With scarcely a tinge of guilt at the sight of leaves scattered all over our lawn, or the work left undone, we followed Duke past our home to wander down our country road. A vision of thousands upon thousands of suburbanites grumbling as they raked leaves and stuffed them into garbage bags, caused me to break out in a cheek-splitting grin.

"What's so funny?" Mary Helen asked.

"We don't have to rake leaves," I replied. "God's wind will rake them for us!"

Raking leaves has always struck me as an unnatural pastime. Now that we live in the country, we can watch them flutter and dance across the lawn without irritation. The autumn wind drifts them into windrows along the borders where the wild field grasses edge our lawn, or across the road into the corn field, or into the woods at the back of our property. If we wait long enough, the yard is blown clean as a golf course. If we wait even longer, the leaves compost the surrounding land. Besides, neighbours aren't close enough to arouse guilt by the swish of their rakes or to give us the evil eye for our failure to do our civic duty.

Not everything joined in the fall flamenco. The leaves on the row of black walnuts had already browned and blown away leaving a squirrel's delight of nuts festooning their branches. White ash stood naked beneath the sky. The saffron dress of the wild cherry was tattered. The odd late-blooming chicory brightened the verge. The goldenrod had faded. The scrubby Manitoba maples were smeared with dirty green and rusty brown. The white pines, however, refused to mourn—shedding their older needles to carpet the edges of our country lane with coffee-coloured straw.

One of our giant friends was mortally wounded. This great pine oozed life from fresh woodpecker stabs. Unseen, carpenter ants were bent on eating out its heart.

It's a time of year when I don't dare have much film for my camera. Each day seems special, each vista a Byzantine mosaic. Along with sunsets and moonlight, Mary Helen has urged me to curtail my love affair with autumn lest overflowing scrapbooks of prints deplete our bank account and stuff our cupboards. But, like rainbows and sunsets, moonbeams and snow scenes, words fail us when we try to describe the subtlety and drama of autumn. Words certainly failed those bards and scribes who attributed all this to "Jack Frost" or "Mother Nature."

Not much better are those who confidently demythologize creation with their "scientific explanation" for autumn's palette.

They remind us each leaf is a food factory in which chlorophyll is a catalyst for the chemical reactions necessary to transform carbon dioxide and water into glucose. All plants contain pigments, hidden by the intense green of spring and summer growth. As the days shorten and the nights grow cooler, green chlorophyll gradually disappears.

With the chlorophyll gone, the leaf can no longer make food. Sunlight reacts on leftover glucose to produce red colours. The leaf colour depends on the degree of sunlight, the amount of glucose left, and the variety of other pigments that are most plentiful in the leaf. Xanthophyll is yellow. Carotene shows itself as orange-red. Anthocyanin creates a red and purple effect.

Understanding some of the reasons why the hillsides wear their colours doesn't lessen the wonder. After all, men have been polluting the earth with their manufacturing for millennia while God's leaf factories have been quietly producing food and enriching the earth from the very beginning. His factories don't pollute, stink, sting the eyes, ruin the water table, de-stabilize the soil, or fill the atmosphere with carbon dioxide. Leaves produce oxygen, not carbon dioxide. Some researchers estimate that one tree purifies as much as forty tons of pollutants in its lifetime! And the visual banquet He spreads!

What a Creator! Not only a Manufacturer without peer and the Perfect Engineering Environmentalist, but an Artist whose skill leaves us searching in vain for words to describe the scenes He paints with such sweeping strokes of His brush. In the words of Robert Service;

> *Have you seen God in His splendours,*
> *heard the text that nature renders?*[35]

Beneath the Great Southern Gooseway

For us of the minority,
the opportunity to see geese
is more important than television,
and the chance to find a pasqueflower is a right
as inalienable as free speech.[36]

We had just smothered our toast with peach jam when we heard it. A faint honk far away. Leaving toast uneaten and coffee to grow cold, we raced outside. We strained our eyes through the pines to the north until we caught sight of a skein of geese high above. Cleaving the country quietness, their wonking pulsed with something primeval. Burnished leaves, brisk winds, and V's of Canada Geese heading south—how we love the autumn.

If they fly down the Great Southern Gooseway (as I have christened it), they pass high above us at an altitude of between 1000 and 3000 feet. Radar has tracked some geese as high as

9500 metres.[37] But if they take the Garden Hill off-ramp to sample a neighbouring farm smorgasbord—as they often do—they fly right over our heads. Then we feel the beat of their powerful wings on our upturned faces.

Their flying formation reflects amazing design. The leader who flies at the apex of the V feels an intense drag as he beats his way through the air. To share the stress, they frequently change positions. The exact shape of their formation allows each bird, except the leader, to benefit from the lift of the bird in front and to see ahead without being blind-sided. This pattern of co-operation enables them to fly much faster and farther than they could if they flew alone or even in a wing formation.

In the late afternoon we drove down to the pond, just in time to watch a flock descend. Like stabilizers on a big jet, their tail feathers fanned out as they came in for a steep, 45 degree landing. With necks stretched forward and wings arching above, their dragging feet hit the water like skis.

Those already there honked their welcome. Canadas carry on almost continuous conversation. Uh-wonk! Uh-wonk! A babble of grunts, snorts, and honks filled the air. Occasionally, when a newcomer invaded a rival's territory, we heard a high-pitched squawk or hiss.

Well over 400 were already cruising the pond after raiding neighbouring stubble fields. Experts tell us there are eight sub-species of Canadas, but to our inexpert eye and weak binoculars, all we could make out were differences in size. We did discover ducks as well: scores of Mallards, a few Black Ducks, and one or two Common Mergansers.

In the dog-leg of the pond, most distant from the road, the geese settled down to catch up on the latest goose gossip. Which fields had the best corn? Which farmer had left the most grain among the stubble? Perhaps they warned each other about danger zones far to the south where hunters waited to bag their limit. More likely, they honked to each other of some distant stretch of pristine lake, some expanse of muskeg, or some rocky land where virgin spruce had never felt the bite of human greed. Most of these would be migrating from Hudson's Bay or Ungava.

The Garden Hill pond used to power a pair of mills when the village was a thriving pioneer settlement. Encircled on three sides by conservation land and forest, it has become home to fish and fowl, two swans, snapping turtles, and a family of ubiquitous beaver. To get a closer look at the geese, we quietly slipped through the cedars along a snaking peninsula that reaches out into the water. With their keen sense of sight and hearing they detected our approach and squawked a warning as they floated away. This was no thunderous retreat of frightened creatures. They sedately sailed away with a disdainful glance in our direction. Somehow a goose bulletin had been circulated that this pond was protected. We settled down to watch.

Another flock descended in formation over the hill only to break up as it approached the pond. They looked like a squadron of aerial acrobats playing up to an exhibition crowd. A few geese did barrel rolls as they spiraled down toward the pond. Some naturalists conjecture that the younger birds like to whiffle; that is, to show off by doing displays of aerobatics. No one really knows for sure—except the geese.

What we do know is more than enough to conclude that Canada Geese can teach us many lessons. Throughout their lives, "Each individual is a member of a pair, a family or a flock—sometimes all three."[38] The great V formations symbolize their commitment to community.

They remind us that we accomplish much more when we work together. That used to be accepted as a fact. Old-fashioned barn raisings mobilized entire rural communities. Long ago, before health insurance, unemployment assistance, and welfare, neighbour helping neighbour was part of rural life. Now, we expect government agencies to care for us, to watch out for our families, and—especially—to be responsible for our neighbours. Technology has made it possible, even in rural areas, to live independent lives. Personal privacy has displaced community. Neighbourliness is so rare that what was once thought commonplace now makes the evening telecast.

Natural disasters periodically rekindle fires of neighbourliness and feed the longing we have for community. In January of 1998, an ice storm of colossal proportions blacked out sections of Eastern Ontario and Quebec. Trees splintered and crashed. Tangled wires and fallen utility poles littered the area. The tons of ice that built up over days of freezing rain even felled great steel towers. The storm of the century provoked an amazing outpouring of continent-wide help and local co-operation. Volunteers manned relief centres day and night.

Cold gripped cities devoid of light and heat. As the situation in rural areas became even grimmer, impatience and anger surfaced—anger not at the ice, but at government utilities. Anger obscured the heroic efforts of workers operating around the clock to try and deal with the decimation of the power grid. It was a kind of anger seldom seen in the Great Depression. Clearly, our reservoir of co-operative action has been seriously depleted by technology and the welfare state. Perhaps the move by governments to downgrade in the face of staggering debts will succeed in inspiring a renewal of volunteerism and community co-operation. That would be a silver lining to a tough lesson— a lesson the geese could have taught us.

These magnificent birds model other virtues as well.

Canada Geese do not believe in divorce; they mate for life. So strong is the pair bond between them that if one is wounded and unable to fly, the mate will abandon the flock to stay with the wounded partner no matter what danger that may pose.[39]

They make superb parents, going to great lengths to protect their offspring. Wildlife painter Robert Bateman, writes: "Canada Geese, for me, are symbols of fidelity and territoriality. I see them as forceful, direct birds." He came to know the male of a pair that nested near his home well enough to feed him out of his hand. "But when I tried to come near their nest in a rubber raft they both charged me with their necks outstretched. The male almost jumped into the raft with me, tried to beat me about the head with his wings, and got me completely soaked."[40]

Their life-long faithfulness mocks our *laissez faire* approach to sex. Throwing fidelity to the winds hardly seems to square with the best we see in nature. Instead of telling someone not to be a silly goose, we should warn them not to be a silly human.

Autumn—season of migrating geese! I'm inclined to agree with Lafe Turluck in John Michener's *Chesapeake*: "The life of

man is divided into two seasons. Geese is here. Geese ain't here."
So, when autumn arrives and we hear the wild sound of their
honking, we still rush outside to gaze heavenward at these great
birds. We do the same in the spring.

> *Wild Geese… are very special birds because their society is based
> on a permanent pair bond and a family life which keeps the
> young with their parents until breeding times come around
> again. …It is more than 50 years since I first fell under their
> spell, and I remain totally addicted to their magic.*[41]

When Wood Warms Twice

Beechwood fires are bright and clear,
If the logs are kept a year.
Chestnut's only good, they say,
If for long it's laid away.
Birch and fir logs burn too fast,
Blaze up bright and do not last.
Elm wood burns like a churchyard mould;
Even the flames are very cold.
Poplar gives a bitter smoke,
Fills your eyes and makes you choke.
Apple wood will scent your room
With an incense like perfume.
Oak and maple, if dry and old,
Keep away the winter's cold.
But ash wood wet, and ash wood dry,
A king shall warm his slippers by.[42]

Mellow October had slipped away. A shrill November wind tore at the stubborn leaves clinging to the oak behind the house. The bite of northern air was beginning to spill down my back where I had loosened my collar to vent the heat rising from my protesting muscles. But as I put down the splitting axe and stood surveying our domain, I sighed, "It doesn't get much better than this."

Light from the rising moon gilded the skeletal trees to the east. A ragged V of Canada Geese honked high overhead. At my feet, all that remained of the pile of logs we had dumped here in early October was sawdust and woodchips. Behind the screen of cedars five cords for the following year stood neatly stacked and covered. By the back door, another five cords of dry wood stood ready to warm us through the winter. "This year I'm ready," I exulted, "We have a system."

The feeling of primeval pride that steals over a country neophyte who has faced down the merciless cold of an approaching winter and prepared for the worst is reserved for those who heat with wood. Lesser mortals who heat with oil or gas can't relate to the elemental struggles the wood-burner faces.

Our first winter here found us unprepared. Wood was hard to find and expensive. I was not totally naïve. I knew the difference between a face cord and a real bush cord, 4 feet x 4 feet x 8 feet, 128 cubic feet of wood. I also knew that oak, maple, and beech deliver the best heat, around 22 million British Thermal Units (BTU's) compared to only 18 for birch. That's about all I knew.

The supplier of split and well-seasoned wood that I contacted, in desperation, saw us as a cash cow. He charged us as if we were city slickers—which we were. I'm sure he thought we were looking for a few face cords to cast a romantic glow on weekends at our country retreat when what we needed was serious wood to keep warm. The price scared us and we bought too little. By late January it was gone. So February found us stumbling through deep snow with an old toboggan fetching meagre loads of cordwood from a distant pile. We tracked snow into the house and we were always short of kindling.

The following year we found a reasonable source and had it delivered early, but I ignored one detail. I failed to tell the supplier that I needed it split. We got a shock when he dumped four cords in our driveway. Out rolled huge, unsplit chunks, cut crosswise from giant maples and oaks. I bought a splitting axe that weighed a ton and got down to work. And so, on through September and October and into the winter, every time I had a few minutes, I attacked those chunks. But after eight years, I still have a few of those giant bolls anchoring a corner of my wood pile.

I soon realized that splitting is an art that has to be learned—and I was in kindergarten. Since the wood had been cut in the late spring, it was still green, and instead of embedding itself in the wood, the axe often bounced off. Dangerous! Learning to let the weight of the axe do the work, and not my arm, gave me serious problems for a while. I kept trying to perfect the knack of swinging the axe in a free arc overhead that landed in just the right place. Too often I misjudged the distance, until I splintered the stout ash handle and had to buy a new one. Determined not to be bested by dumb wood, I stubbornly attacked every knot until I learned by hard experience to give them a wide berth.

Before long, I could classify wood into splitting categories; "piece of cake," "not bad," "needs a serious smack," "stupid wood," and "impossible." When smitten in the right place, beech and oak split evenly and easily. Both yellow and white birch, ash and black cherry join oak in this category. Second comes maple, which can be stubborn, especially where swirls and knots abound. The fibres of some woods, such as ironwood, seem so intertwined that splitting is murder. The big chunks of oak and maple, however, resisted every effort until I bought a couple of wedges. Even so, it took several years before I discovered that instead of trying to split the whole boll in two, it was better to attack the edges. The younger sapwood could be split off the outside of these chunks in narrow slabs.

The splitting took so long that year, that we were lugging wood in the most awful weather, through rain and sleet and snow. But worst of all, it wasn't dry enough. It continually frustrated our attempts to get it burning well enough to throw off a good heat.

The third year, I was sure I had the problem licked. To supplement the dry cords of oak and maple left from the previous year's struggles, I ordered a huge load of hardwood slabs from a nearby sawmill. Slabs are the half-round pieces left after lumber is cut from a log. I congratulated myself on getting both dry, burnable wood, and kindling at one fell swoop. Cheap! Unfortunately, a busy spell in September and October kept me from attacking the pile. Then a sudden storm in early November buried it under snow that lasted all winter. I spent spare time during the next two months digging out frozen slabs, cutting them to size, and lugging them to the back door. What I hadn't counted on, and what Mary Helen kept reminding me about, was the sawdust that clung to the frozen slabs until I brought them inside. We seemed to find sawdust everywhere, even in our cereal. Finally I gave up. But every time I backed the car out, that ominous mound of slabs mocked me. Mary Helen didn't have to say a word.

By the fourth year, I realized that I badly needed a system to cheat the weather. In our first year, I planted grapevines on either side of the back door. They had begun to give us a bumper crop that Mary Helen transformed into delicious juice. I could envision a grape arbour covered with luscious fruit extending back from the mud room over the patio. Then the idea hit me that an arbour could fulfill two functions. Grapes and shade during the summer, shelter for wood during the winter. Eureka! That year I put up the framework for the arbour. We piled our winter's supply of wood under the arbour and covered the whole contraption with a couple of tarps. Presto, we had a dry shelter right at the back door that allowed us to fetch wood in the worst weather. Fine until several real storms blew our tarps to pieces. I would have to make our wood shelter more wind resistant.

But I was beginning to develop a system. Order split oak and maple from 100 miles north where the price is reasonable. Cajole the woodsman to deliver it in late August, rather than late October. Call after call required! In early October, pile the seasoned wood from the previous year under the arbour and stack the new wood in a pile for next year. And instead of bringing nests of mice inside in boxes of kindling, store it in barrels with tight lids. By this time we had also bought a Vermont Castings airtight stove that didn't warp and threw out enough heat to warm the whole of our open-concept house.

Last year it all came together. We declared a "wood festival" and invited some choice friends to a dinner with all the fixin's. Catch? Come and help us cut, haul, and pile wood. I bought a mound of logs from a neighbour for half the price I paid the previous year. But, although dry, I needed it cut and transported down the road to our house and I had no truck. (I haven't convinced Mary Helen yet that all country dwellers need a truck.) Fortunately, several friends with more enlightened spouses came on a Saturday in early October. One even brought a pick-up loaded with construction scraps to use for kindling. By the end of the day, five or six cords of wood lay piled at the end of our driveway. After a roast beef dinner, we waved our friends on their way—tired, aching, and exhilarated that they had helped their country cousins prepare for the winter. I didn't learn till later that one came down with a powerful case of poison ivy. I don't think he'll come next year.

By early November I had cut, split, and stacked the whole pile, most of it to season for the following year. The wood from the previous year we piled at the back door under the grape arbour. By this time I had designed a frame-work to attach to the arbour and cover with tarps in such a way that the shelter would resist any storm. We also filled the mud room with a reserve pile accessible on the coldest days. With a couple of barrels full of kindling, we faced the winter with equanimity.

I surveyed our domain. The driveway was clear, even of wood chips. Five cords of wood for next year stood in a neat pile behind the cedars. Inside my arbour-shelter, another five cords of wood waited for winter's worst. I was five or ten pounds lighter, and felt 100 percent fitter. My middle-aged paunch had receded noticeably. Heating with wood has many benefits. It promotes health, is reasonable in cost, and it warms the woodsman twice!

Author splitting wood.

Does Anyone Love November?

O wild West Wind, thou breath of Autumn's being,
Thou, from whose unseen presence the leaves dead
Are driven, like ghosts from an enchanter fleeing,
Yellow, and black, and pale, and hectic red,
Pestilence-stricken multitudes.[43]

W e woke to the sound of rain drumming on the roof: not April showers, not a drought-busting July torrent—a bone-chilling November deluge. It had already drizzled for three days. My joints ached as I made my way downstairs through the chilly house to peer outside at the grayness. "This will not be a good day," I thought.

Away from home a lot that fall, I had set aside this specific Saturday to catch up on outdoor work. Stuck to the fridge by those ridiculous little magnets we all collect, the list looked daunting: last-minute caulking, garden to tidy, roses to hill, lawnmower to put away, item after item—things I should have done a month ago.

It's November. Optimism has fled. Summer days are a memory. The golden garments of autumn lie wet and ugly beneath the naked trees. Winter's snowy gown may soon be woven, but November's drab coat has no ermine fringe. Spring is beyond hope.

Re-scheduling my workload, I set aside another day at home in the week ahead to prepare for winter. But that whole week crept by full of drizzle and fog, downpours and cold. Trying to juggle travel with duties at home left my schedule in tatters. I was in a blue funk.

I like to set deadlines—sometimes even impossible deadlines. They stretch me and, I must admit, make me feel rather smug when I accomplish tasks no one thought I could. Often that means over-scheduling, but isn't that what being a man is all about? Goal-orientation. Satisfaction from an impossible job completed. Life marked out like a highway with road signs of completed tasks. Okay, my to-do list sometimes leads me around by the nose like a bull being led to the slaughter. I have even trampled a few relationships by charging ahead. But...

"Mary Helen will not be happy with another postponement of household promises," I muttered to myself. "Not my fault. Been raining for days—and I've got commitments, don't I?"

Heading out on a trip that morning, I stopped for gas. "Isn't this miserable weather," Fred mumbled as rain dripped off his cap. "You can say that again!" I responded to our local gas jockey.

Everybody complained about the weather that week. They blamed El Niño or La Niña. They criticized the weatherman. Some seemed ready to lay it at the feet of Parliament. Most of all, they faulted November.

In temperate zones there seems to be a universal animosity towards November. When the novelist Georges Simenon wanted a setting that would depict misery and mystery in the life of a family outside Paris, he chose a rainy November. Indeed, the title he gave to his psychological tale of family horror was—you guessed it—*November*.[44]

As I drove east, I pondered my attitude toward the weather. I knew that grumbling would not improve it. Railing against the weather is like shouting at Niagara Falls. Why then don't I just accept it and get on with life? I suppose part of the reason has to do with conversation. Complaints about the weather are safe gambits to throw into the conversational stewpot. How can I talk to strangers—let alone acquaintances—if I don't grumble about the weather? Without a dash of complaint, the stew might seem tasteless.

Surely there is more to this quirk than conversational penury. Do we perceive our inability to control the weather as a threat to our independence? Can we trace our irritability to our failure to program the climate like we govern the atmosphere in our homes? Is this why storm clouds can so quickly blacken our moods?

The wipers beat a dirge as I mused, "Is the weather miserable or am I miserable?" Although we all realize the futility of complaining about the elements, we all do it. And yet it shows up our humanity in such a poor light. It challenges our arrogance, exposes our ego, and tries our patience. Of course, our attitude toward the weather is not new. In 1877, John Burroughs wrote, 'I was born with a chronic anxiety about the weather."[45]

As the rain began to lessen, I considered this phobia. In spite of circling satellites and hourly bulletins, the weather remains mysterious. It angers us. It threatens our self-sufficiency. It laughs at our control fetish. Perhaps the march of technology has spoiled us so badly, we actually believe we should be able to conquer this natural foe and order it to deliver good weather on demand. If we can't afford a holiday on the Costa Del Sol aren't sunny days our egalitarian right?

Miserable weather either drives me to a good book or awakens in me the frustrated philosopher. Since I couldn't read and drive, I continued to wax philosophical about the effect of weather on my sense of contentment. When contentment flees, frustration "ravels the sleeve of care." My sleeve was quite raveled that day! But in acceptance of the weather, and other givens of life, I could knit a coverlet of serenity that would help to prepare me for life's really tough times.

In order to knit that coverlet, I need to consciously accept what I cannot change—whether it be weather, annoying people, or affliction. Alexander Whyte, an old Scots preacher, practiced perpetual thankfulness. His attitude amazed his parishioners. But one cold and rainy Sunday, they thought he would be stumped. However, when he stood to pray, he began, "We thank thee Lord, that it is not always like this."

By this time I was more than half way to my destination. I determined to stop complaining and accept what I couldn't change. Having stilled resentment's dirge, I wondered if there was anything to be thankful for in the November scenery drifting by. I began to look more closely. Dogwood stems lent splashes of burgundy to the lowlands where willows radiated yellow warmth. Paper birch supported fans of wine filigree. Red fruit festooned a wild apple tree. Milkweed pods trailed streamers of parachutes.

As the rain ceased and the mist dissipated, the landscape projected a beauty I had never seen. Here and there, evergreens softened the edge of the woodlands where the hardwoods stood exposed. But instead of seeing a chaotic jumble of branches, they became a gossamer gown clothing the naked hills.

A row of white pines stood silhouetted against the sky. They all leaned away from the prevailing wind. On the northwest side their branches were stunted and twisted while on the southeast they looked like the bony arms of mothers pleading for their refugee children, or could it be dancers in a ballet?

The earth's physique lay spread out before me. Autumn's vivid wardrobe had been set aside to unveil the undulating beauty of the land. November became a nightgown woven with subtleties of texture and tint invisible until now. The scantily clad earth waited for winter to spread its blanket over the land. I felt like a bridegroom catching the first glimpse of his virgin bride in her negligée. Why had I not noticed November's beauty before?

> *Were I not cold how should I come to know*
> *One potent pleasure of the sun's sweet rays?*
> *Or did I never breast the driving snow*
> *What bliss were sweetest kernel of June days?*[46]

Mary Helen, Cailie, and Duke.

WINTER

First Snow

Snow—snow—fast-falling snow!
Snow on the house-tops—snow in the street
Snow overhead, and snow under feet.
Snow in the country—snow in the town,
Silently, silently sinking down;
Everywhere, everywhere fast-falling snow,
Dazzling the eyes with its crystalline glow![47]

December found us wistfully looking through the window for any sign of falling flakes. Instead, the road was a snake slithering through the valley. It bled brown blood where it cut through the hills. The green coverlet that hid the wrecks scattered around the barns on the next concession had been thrown back. Rusting where they were abandoned decades ago, trucks, tractors, cars, manure spreaders, a harvester, and dozens of other unidentified hulks leered at us from beneath the naked trees. Cattle shuffled through the mud. The world was brown and grey.

The wind changed. The Snow Maker on high waved his wand. Snow began to fall. He dressed the rusting wrecks in wool. He trimmed the houses and barns in ermine. The ditches and fields were carpeted and the branches of the leafless hardwoods frosted with white. He hung up the evergreen dress of the pines and spruce, helping them into gowns of white lace. With prodigal delight he touched the tiniest plants. Snow spilled from the milkweed pods like sand from a cockle shell. Snow gilded the red berries of the wild rose and the hanging streamers of grapevine. Winter put Brown and Grey to sleep beneath a blanket of purest wool.

Birds that had been gleaning the fields, returned to our yard. Merry chickadees swarmed the suet ball. Blue jays scattered inferior tidbits in their search for sunflower seeds. Nuthatches dive-bombed the feeders. Juncos crisscrossed the snow as they scavenged for fallen seed.

Softness enveloped the ragged landscape. Bushes and grasses became feathery fronds. A dusting of white velvet coated unsightly buildings. Magically, shacks became mansions; parked clunkers, chariots.

The sparkle that snow brings to Mary Helen's eyes, beckoned me forth from my lair. Donning parkas, we headed outdoors where we wandered like children through a world transformed. Duke bounded down the hill to join us with snowflakes decorating his black nose. He leapt to catch a snowball. When Mary Helen spied a pine branch loaded with snow she lured me beneath it so she could shower me with snow and watch the branch spring free.

Both of us love snow—without being skiers or snowmobilers and without Mary Helen being able to stand up on ice. She grew up in eastern South Carolina where a serious snowfall occurs scarcely once in a decade or two. On the other hand, snowmen, snow forts, snowball fights, and skating on a local creek were part of my childhood. Diverse in our background, we unite to cheer, "Let it snow, let it snow, let it snow!"

In the valley skiers waxed their skis. Snowmobilers checked their machines. Like many other aspects of country living, however, you don't have to spend money to maximize enjoyment. The snow itself is a delight. Down in the town, our granddaughters would be making snow angels. Lying down in the snow and moving their hands and feet from side to side, they would leave behind an angel shape before leaping up to chase each other through the snow.

Quietness had descended with the snow. It muted Duke's bark and muffled the bawl of a heifer. It even stilled the occasional rumble of a truck on the county road. Tranquillity reigned… until we were arrested in our ramblings by the roar of engines straining to climb the hill near our house. Suddenly, the mad motorcyclist, metamorphosed by the sight of snow into a crazy snowmobiler, hurtled over the top of the hill. A bevy of other snowmobiles followed him down the road toward us. Soiling the white mantle with flung gravel and mud, they raced by with a high-pitched whine and friendly waves. We didn't feel very friendly, knowing as we did that the sign at the bottom of the steep hill read, "No motorized vehicles." Offended by their invasion, Duke tore after them barking wildly. We didn't even try to stop him.

But who can be irritated long in the presence of freshly fallen snow? Shafts of sunlight filtering through the scudding clouds struck sparks of light off the glistening snow. A coronation robe shimmering with diamonds had replaced the dingy garb of brown and grey. Each speck of snow is a separate wonder, an ice crystal formed around a speck of dust. These six-sided marvels form symmetrical stars, needles, and columns. Although transparent, reflection from their multiple surfaces makes them appear white. Partially melted crystals stick to each other to form the snowflakes used by the Creator to knit winter's coat.

Understandably, not all view snow with wonder! Ten miles south of us, commuters crept along deep in slush. They peered through windshields caked with grime. Arriving home late for supper, they grumbled as they shoveled snow from their driveways. Inside, they collapsed in front of suppers rendered tasteless and dry by delay while they scanned the Travel Section for bargains in Arizona and Florida. "Why doesn't winter just go away?"

Twilight stole across valley and hillside, but deep darkness was held at bay by skylight reflected off a trillion crystals of snow. Snow banishes the blackness of night, fracturing it into multiplied shades of inky blue. In winter, the palette of the Great Artist contains hitherto unknown tints of indigo, ultramarine, cobalt, and ebony. To walk at night through a snowy countryside with only starlight to light the way, is—to me—one of life's most poignant experiences. And when the moon rises over new fallen snow, the beauty is so breathtaking that one can almost see the gates of heaven. Trees and buildings and fencerows become indigo shadows washed with silver in a surrealist mural of serenity.

The blanket of mysterious peace that snow throws over our psyche has been experienced by many. Writing in *The Place in the Forest*, R.D. Lawrence traces his forest epiphany to a walk he took after a snowstorm:

> *Before me, beyond the boundaries of the land that I owned, stretched a white forest that knew not the taint of human weaknesses. No evil lurked ahead; there was none to lie, or steal, or cheat; here there were no fine speeches cloaking the lust for power, or greed; no blood would be spilled here needlessly, uselessly. Why did I think thus then? Why do I think thus now, as I write of this day that has passed? Perhaps the peace of mind that came to me out there reached into hidden recesses of the mind... perhaps. I know not. But I felt alive on that day; alive and glad that I had found this wilderness and I think now that if there ever was a time of demarcation... that time occurred on that day.*[48]

Although the splinters of human hope lie scattered everywhere, snow breeds optimism. Blanketing everything with gentle whiteness, snow can invigorate the soul in a way little else, except perhaps spring, can do. Not that snow makes any permanent changes in the landscape. What is hidden will eventually come to light. It does, however, cover ugliness and clutter. It brightens. It softens. It dampens noise. And, as Ontario's pioneers knew from experience, "A year of snow makes apples grow."[49]

If only human prodigality could be covered as easily as the brown and grey of winter! On a broad front, unlikely; on an individual level, quite possible. The blanket of white is a token from the Great Snow Maker of a covering much more durable.

No wonder we love the snow. If we don't have to drive often over icy roads, we seldom get too much. Some winters, like last year, there was not nearly enough of that white, soft, quiet, glistening, playful snow. We perk up whenever it covers the dormant land with its blanket of beauty. We sulk when it disappears—but we may be unusual.

> *Here winter's breath is rude*
> *His fingers cold and wan;*
> *But what's his wildest mood*
> *To the tyranny of man?*[50]

Sipping Soup and Saving Money

The Crown of the House is Godliness.
The Beauty of the House is Order.
The Glory of the House is Hospitality.
The Blessing of the House is Contentment.[51]

(Inscription over a pioneer fireplace)

With thoughts of supper urging him on, Duke bounded ahead of us on the return leg of our walk and disappeared down his driveway. We continued on. When our home came in sight, hunger caused us to quicken our pace.

As soon as we opened the door, the aroma of soup and the warmth from our wood stove enveloped us in their embrace. Somehow, soup and country living go together. Ever since our move we have been expanding our soup-making repertoire. Each of us have our specialties. I concentrate on hearty soups like vegetable-beef, ten-bean, and cabbage. Mary Helen prepares a more refined product; Chinese chicken corn soup, beef and barley soup, broccoli soup, split pea soup, and Carolina vegetable soup. Makes my mouth water to write about them.

On the day in question, we ladled cabbage soup into our bowls and headed over to the wood stove to get warm. This is lumberjack soup, almost as thick as stew. With faces rosy from the wind and a tremor registering 6.5 on the hunger scale shaking our insides, conversation died away as we tucked in.

Earlier I had taken a break from writing to add carrots, potatoes, tomatoes, barley, green pepper, celery, and cabbage to sautéed onions, garlic, hamburg, and spices. Then I left it to simmer slowly while we went for a walk.

Hearing that we were coming into town to visit, our son John put in his request. "Mom, have you any of that pea soup?" Pea soup, like the French Canadians make it, is my wife's domain. He had heard, via the grapevine, that we had recently served guests baked ham. He knew the pattern.

Ill-prepared for winter—our son John helps to bring wood in by toboggan in first year.

When hams go on sale, we pick up several to keep in the freezer. Guests for dinner? No problem. Out comes a ham with the best slices reserved for the guests and the leftovers earmarked for soup. The day after a dinner party, Mary Helen simmers the ham bone, strains the broth and adds leftover bits of ham to sautéed onions along with a pound or two of green split peas. Um, good! I usually try to pilfer some of the broth and leftover ham to add to my ten-bean soup.

For other soups we make beef broth from soup bones. Mary Helen cooks up a big pot of broth, to which she adds onions and whatever vegetable is reasonable. Strained and put away in small containers in the freezer, we always have broth available to add to any of our soups. Frozen in this way, skimming off the fat before use is easy. During harvest we also flash freeze tomatoes and chopped green pepper to add to our dishes. Instead of buying stewing beef for beef soups, we look for sales on a more reasonable cut like blade steak. If it has a bone, so much the better. The bone adds flavour.

When I cook my soup, I usually prepare curry as well. To sautéed garlic and onion, I add cut-up blade steak, hamburg, or chicken seasoned with an equal amount of chili pepper and turmeric plus a dash of ginger. As it simmers, I add some of our broth and a couple of frozen, broken-up tomatoes. After several hours of simmering I put it away in small portions in the freezer. Then, whenever we get a hankering for something spicy, we can add a seasonal vegetable to the curry base. Voilà—chicken and pea curry, or hamburg and spinach, or beef and cauliflower—the combinations are endless. Along with the curry, we'll either have rice pilau (pilaf) or nan. Of course, not everyone likes the tantalizing aroma of these dishes, so we have to be careful to ventilate the house well whenever guests are due.

Large pots of homemade soup and curry base help us to reduce the bottom line while promoting a healthy lifestyle. By cooking our own, we can avoid using salt, skim off the fat, and maximize the use of vegetables. Having a variety of soups and curries in the freezer simplifies the planning of reasonable meals and saves a great deal of time. We also have extra to share with family or shut-ins. Living on less certainly does not mean having boring meals.

When we left a secure job to venture forth on our own, we knew we would have to economize. A scary thought. As it turned out, one of the benefits of country living has been an impetus to simplify our lives and reduce our expenditures. An unexpected dividend has been the discovery that living on less leads to a richer life.

Kicking the consumer habit and winning the financial war is a campaign of small victories waged against a ubiquitous foe. Advertising assails us from every quarter. Our mailboxes get stuffed with it. Our ears are bombarded by it. Our eyes are blinded by it. Flyers, billboards, radios, TV, magazines, newspapers, even the world-wide web—all *scream*, whisper, wheedle, threaten, plead with us to buy.

Unbridled consumption, however, spawns a multitude of maladies. When we first moved to the country, I was still suffering from Canadiantireitis, an ailment afflicting a large proportion of Canadian males. It is distinguished by a fever that appears with the arrival of the Canadian Tire advertising flyer.

Canadian Tire is the Canadian hybrid of stores like Walmart and Kmart, but with a peculiar masculine appeal: a million kinds of screw drivers, tools for everything, ingenious new gadgets, skis, electronics, doohickies for the car, whatchamacallits for the hunter or the fisherman, and household necessities. Something is always on sale! Not only that, but to soothe your conscience for wasting money on some useless gadget, you get Canadian Tire coupons that are as good as money on the next purchase.

I got hooked! Every week, I would pounce on the flyer and look for things I convinced myself I needed. I would point out to Mary Helen that we couldn't afford not to stock up at those sale prices. I acquired more screw drivers than a mechanic, more drill bits than I can ever use, a nifty little picture-frame-fixer that I've never been able to work, tubes of glue in their original packaging, a dozen rolls of aluminum foil. I had a bad case. Since I couldn't find a local branch of Consumers Anonymous to help me kick Canadiantireitis, I went through painful withdrawal. I still feel a spasm when the flyer arrives.

Canadiantireitis is but one strain of the virus, *materiensus consumerosis*. Americans contract *Walmartitis*. Every country has its own strain. The virus muddles our reason to the point that we convince ourselves that what we would like, is actually what we need. "The Smiths have a new car and our clunker is a disgrace to the neighbourhood." "Everyone has a cell phone. I might need one in an emergency." There is always a new kind of exotic food, a brand-name blouse, new carpet, an addition to the house, new shoes, a big screen TV, a trip to Europe, a snowmobile, a bigger house. a computer update, a new CD…

Today's Garden of Eden is cleverly disguised as a shopping mall where every shop offers us a taste of "forbidden fruit" on easy terms. Zero interest! No money down! Special layaway plan! Using our freedom to slap down plastic whenever we see something we want, we sow prodigally, and reap a ball and chain of debt. Then comes overtime work, extra jobs, years of payments, absentee parenting—worries by the barrel.

Epicurus said, "If you want to make a man happy, add not to his possessions, but take away from his desires." So, while every billboard from Hollywood to cyberspace is designed to inflame our desires, our goal should be their domestication. This is much easier said than done—one reason happiness is so rare in our culture, a society in which more people have more possessions than at any other time in history.

In our case, necessity forced us to wrestle the consumer impulse to the mat. By buying attractive, good quality clothes that last. By mixing and matching them with what we already had. By extending the life of our car—now twelve years old. By making our own fun—enjoying the snow without a snowmobile or elaborate ski attire, exploring the villages and towns around, celebrating the passage of the seasons.

The struggle to replace feverish consumption by peaceful contentment is a fight worth waging. Contentment domesticates our desires. It enables us to defer gratification. It stifles avarice and envy. And since we don't have to earn as much to feed our habit, we don't have to work at two jobs. It leaves us with more time to do worthwhile things. Blessed are they who value contentment over consumption! Of course, the struggle is never completely over.

> *More and more, young families are seeking their leisure and recreation in activities which are quiet, use muscles instead of motors, and—where possible—can be done "far from the madding crowd." The beauty of it all is that many of these activities can be enjoyed at minimum cost. There never has been a price put on a sunset. Or moonrise.*[52]

> *Look at the birds of the air… See how the lilies of the field grow…*
> *Do not worry about your life, what you will eat or drink;*
> *or about your body, what you will wear.*
> *Is not life more important than food,*
> *and the body more important than clothes?*[53]

---

*Most of the luxuries, and many of the so called comforts of life,
are not only not indispensable,
but positive hindrances to the elevation of mankind.
With respect to luxuries and comforts,
the wisest have ever lived a more simple
and meagre life than the poor.* [54]

Author and his most recent grandson, Nathan.

Country Christmas

O little town of Bethlehem,
How still we see thee lie!
Above thy deep and dreamless sleep
The silent stars go by.
Yet in thy dark streets shineth
The everlasting Light;
The hopes and fears of all the years
Are met in thee tonight.

Until credit card anxiety smothered my childhood delight in Christmas, the season was magical. Decorating the tree. Hiding Christmas presents. Opening Christmas cards. The cards I loved most depicted snowbound villages with children skating on frozen ponds or sleighs jingling down country lanes. No wonder some of my happiest childhood memories are of Christmas in the country. Every three years or so, we would make a pilgrimage to the country to celebrate our extended family's annual get-together at one of the farms of my country cousins. They did have frozen ponds—and cows and horses and pigs and mysterious, cavernous barns full of cobwebs and fragrant hay and pungent farm scents.

Finally, almost fifty years later I was there, immersed in a country Christmas. Lights illuminated a manger scene in front of Dorothy's House Museum. Three angels, proclaiming "peace on earth," adorned the snow in front of the village church. Christmas trees hid Gary's store. Candles cast a warm glow from several village windows. The row of houses north of the gas station blazed with a bewildering array of lights and decorations: Christmastime in Northumberland County.

On a crisp day in early December, with the grandchildren in tow, I set out to search for the perfect cut-your-own Christmas tree. We came up empty at two Christmas tree farms. Finally, we explored a third on County Road 10. Like kids in a candy store we wandered up and down the rows of pines and spruce. "What about that one?" Adrianna queried. "Too big," I replied.

"Here's one," shouted Kassandra. We circled it critically, before discarding it as too small.

A hundred trees later, Shareena pointed to a white spruce. It was a beauty—right size, fragrant, symmetrical. "Perfect," I decreed, running to fetch the bow saw.

Cutting it took a couple of minutes. Lugging it to the car, stuffing it into the trunk, and tying it down took twenty. But hey, I'd saved five bucks and connected with Debbie's three girls. Manoeuvring it through the front door, scattering needles all over the carpet, wrestling with the rusty stand, untangling the lighting nightmare, wedging folded pieces of paper under the stand to make the tree stand straight—these took the edge off my Christmas nostalgia.

However, the clean scent of spruce wafting through the house went far towards restoring my mood. A visit Mary Helen and I took to Millbrook did the rest. The village in the valley below looked like a Christmas card remembered from childhood—church steeples, millpond, Victorian brick stores. We descended the steep hill onto the main street where coloured lights cast a warm glow. A group of carolers led by Santa Claus had gathered under a street light to sing:

Joy to the world
The Lord has come.
Let earth receive her king!

Ah... the wonder of Christmas! We ambled from store to store sampling hot mulled cider and goodies. We meandered past families sharing candy apples. Here and there, we picked up last-minute presents. Two great Clydesdales lumbered by with a wagon load of children. Soon, we proceeded to the Legion Hall where actors from the Fourth Line Theatre put on an impromptu concert. In spite of microphone problems and restless children, they regaled us with impersonations of Scrooge:

A donation to help the poor at Christmas?
Humbug! Why don't you send them all to the poor house?

They brought readings, sang Irish songs, and led us in the inspiring music of Christmas:

Hark the herald angels sing
Glory to the newborn King!

Silent Night, Holy Night,
All is calm, all is bright...

O little town of Bethlehem,
How still we see thee lie,
The hopes and fears of all the years
Are met in thee tonight.

It would have been a blissful country Christmas—but that was the year Mary Helen backed me into a corner. Oh, I had it coming. Early in the year, I had made one too many caustic comments about my wife's penchant for beginning to buy Christmas presents after Easter. With wifely indignation, she dumped the whole job in my lap. Our grown children and their kids bore witness as she solemnly assigned me the job of buying presents for the whole year. Birthdays. Anniversaries. Christmas. I knew I was in trouble. With no honourable way to back out and retain my male dignity, I had been forced to nonchalantly reply, "Hardly fair, but okay. No problem." Little did I imagine the challenge I faced.

When friends heard about it, they hooted. After their laughter died down, the men frowned their displeasure at my betrayal of their gender. The women purred.

And so began the year of omnipresent presents. With six granddaughters and one grandson, I soon came unraveled. The little darlings informed me how much they liked clothes. With birthdays throughout the year, I was doomed to wandering through the children's departments in sundry stores in search of jumpers and blouses, tights and dresses. Even when my wife took a little pity on me, the task seemed hopeless. Bewildered, I settled on an alternate plan of attack. I would steer clear of children's clothing and concentrate on toys. No problem with the grandson, but the dolls left me bewildered: wetting dolls, crying dolls, dolls with names, dolls with outfits, boy dolls, girl dolls... Then there were all the animal dolls!

Christmas raced toward me. My usual practice of waiting until a day or two before Christmas was not going to work. My list was like lead in my pocket. I felt ominously out-of-sorts. My mood bordered on that of the mother who stepped into an elevator in a busy department store. Her children were crying and clutching her coat. Her arms were loaded with presents. She remarked loudly, "Who invented Christmas anyway? He ought to have been shot."

A man replied quietly from the back of the elevator, "You don't have to worry, ma'am, they crucified him." The elevator noticeably quieted.

Hum. I would have to get on top of things. I could hardly give my Christmas homily with that kind of an attitude—especially since I had used that very vignette in a sermon the year before.

Meanwhile, as grandparents, we had serious duties to perform. There were two Christmas pageants to attend. Each pageant approached the central miracle of Christmas from a fresh perspective. Each injected hilarity that made grown-ups, stressed out by shopping and schedules, laugh uproariously.

The first, at the school, evoked loud applause from assorted parents, uncles, aunts, and grandparents even when the children sang off-key. Comic relief went far beyond the printed program. An angel on the right almost fell off the stage. A pigtailed waif stopped in mid song, crawled on all fours behind the carolers, and jumped off the stage to ask her teacher in a loud whisper to take her to the washroom. On the left, a five-year-old cherub practicing for a career in mime, made faces at his more sombre playmates, bounced up and down, and waved his arms like a bird about to take off.

At our daughter's church, a heart-warming story of two city slickers discovering the real meaning of Christmas from some country cousins proceeded like a Hollywood production—until the last scene. The cast, all decked out in country duds, sang of the birth of Jesus with a country twang. Then the dangerous point in any production arrived. Kindergarten angels and shepherds marched onto the platform. Three boys carried cotton sheep under their arms. Chaos descended as they vied for positions near the manger by beating each other over the head with their sheep. The audience soared aloft on billows of laughter until the harried producers restored order. The Lord himself smiled on the scene.

In spite of my Christmas-list troubles, I felt good. Christmas was here again. The family would come home for the weekend. Church bells would ring. Candles would be lit. The story would be retold. Beyond the crowds of stressed-out shoppers there is a history that nothing can displace. Children repeat it. Carolers sing it. Crèches display it. For a moment at Christmas, the whole universe seems to breathe a sigh of hope.

I came through that Christmas a much wiser man. I learned to pave the year with praise for Mary Helen's far-sighted approach to Christmas buying. And, like Scrooge, I said to myself, "I will honour Christmas in my heart, and try to keep it all the year." [55]

> Give each new day its own good cheer
> And other days apart,
> And every day throughout the year
> Keep Christmas in your heart. [56]

A January Roller Coaster

My feelings at the coming of winter have changed recently.
Once I was oppressed with the forebodings of
"the dreary season";
now, while yet I regret losing the soft beauties of autumn,
still winter fills me with a new excitement,
different to that which I feel on the eve of spring,
yet it is strong, vigorous,
and I mourn not for the autumn and look forward
to this virile new time.
This change within me was caused by The Place
and it began on that Sunday morning
when Joan and I left our car
and began to walk through the snow,
climbing the slope that leads now to our cabin.[57]

I n the pre-dawn stillness, as I sleepily scooped coffee into the coffee maker, I distinctly heard the sound of dripping water. The light from the kitchen window glinted off drops of water falling from the frozen eavestrough. I stumbled over to the window and peered into the darkness. I squinted to read the thermometer. Yes, the mercury was definitely above zero. A thaw!

After a warm and leisurely fall, winter had conquered—catching us unprepared in early November. A busy schedule and soothing fall weather had lulled us into benign neglect of our outdoor duties. The rose bushes shivered unhilled. Mounds of firewood lay unpiled. Stalks of corn and clumps of Brussel sprouts stared accusingly from under the early snow. We had quickly abandoned them to their icy fate. Arctic air, like a hoard of Mongol warriors, chased us into our winter hideaway. Blow after blow of its mailed fist hammered us with alternating blizzards and ice-storms through November and into December. The ground lay imprisoned under a foot of snow covering a thick layer of ice. Humps of ice ridged our walk and driveway.

Then, in mid-January, a reprieve. Throughout the day the eavestroughs began to thaw. The snowcap on our roof shrank. The sidewalk re-appeared. Rivulets of water coursed down our driveway. As night fell, a steady rain loosened winter's grip.

The next morning, we woke to a verdant vision. Like flash-frozen beans thawing in the microwave, patches of unbelievably green grass appeared. Loosed from snowy slumber, herbs and perennials seemed ready to flourish and flower.

Like a hibernating bear woken too abruptly from wintry dreams, the freshet on one side of our property began to roar and grumble. Trickles of melted snow from the field across the road gushed through the culvert. Far downstream, chunks of ice poured over the mill dam on the Ganaraska slamming like bumper cars into trees and each other in their headlong rush to the lake.

Then the wind shifted. Between lunch and supper, I watched the thermometer plunge from ten above to ten below. The trickles and puddles on our laneway congealed. The driveway in front of the garage became a rink. We threw more logs on the fire and expunged from our minds fanciful ideas of an early spring. Such mental cleansing is necessary in a Canadian winter.

Around 1885, James Gay remarked about the fickleness of our climate:

Canadian climate must have been changeable
ever since the world begun,
One hour snowing, and the next raining like fun,
Our blood sometimes thick, other times thin,
This is the time colds begin.[58]

A day later, driving home, we crept through a white-out as Arctic air flung streamers of snow horizontally across our path. The temperature dipped even lower. Winter's icy fist held us more firmly in its clutches.

Three days after the thaw, we peered out the front window wistfully. We knew we should walk for our health, but the thermometer registered minus 20 degrees centigrade! In the west a fan of feathery clouds filtered the dying rays of the setting sun. Ripples of carmine and violet tinted the snow-clad fields beckoning us to venture forth. "Honey, let's try even if we only go a short distance," my southern wife pleaded. Feeling my northern blood stir under the challenge, I muttered, "Why not?"

Thick socks. Long johns. An extra sweater. Toque and scarf. After wrestling on our wintry garb, we gingerly stepped out into the frosty air. Skirting the icy driveway, we headed east down a track through the silent woods beneath a waxing moon which cast silvery streamers of frigid light through the tracery of overarching maple and oak. Here and there, pine and spruce were silhouetted like cerulean soldiers from some long-forgotten battle frozen in time by the ghostly orb.

Beneath our feet, the snow gave off the peculiar *scrunch, scrunch* that heralds sub-zero cold. A dusting of recent snow almost obscured the tracks of deer and rabbits that bisected our path. The cold scorched our tonsils and nipped our noses. Despite the bite of arctic air, I breathed a sigh of deep satisfaction. Out here in the quiet woods everything seemed so pristine, so distant from the proud and persistent pettiness that blares from the tube and screams from the rag. The insistent sale papers that stuff our mailbox seemed laughably irrelevant. Even the beer cans and candy wrappers, left by careless hikers, that would become visible in the spring were hidden by the forgiving snow. We walked on, feeling "the wild witchery of the winter woods."[59]

By the time we finally turned towards home, the pale light of the rising moon had transformed the snow along our path into translucent waves of palest sapphire. The sky in the west had darkened into deep indigo shot through with strands of cobalt and magenta. The warm glow from two windows of a farmhouse beckoned across a distant field. The bawl of a heifer shivered the silence. Winter twilight darkened the fields and crept down the hill to enfold our log home. Warmth from the glowing wood stove embraced us as we entered.

Winter in the country is no ogre chaining us in despair until spring. We find instead, the divine Artist often lures us outdoors to wander awestruck through his gallery of ever-changing murals, even in what we—when anesthetized—had called the *dead* of winter.

*The inhabitants of cities suppose that the country landscape
is pleasant only half the year.
I please myself with observing the graces of the winter scenery,
and believe that we are as much touched by it
as by the genial influence of summer.
To the attentive eye, each moment of the year has its own beauty,*

and in the same field, it beholds, every hour,
a picture which was never seen before,
and which shall never be seen again.
The heavens change every moment,
and reflect their glory or gloom on the plains beneath.[60]

Winter fun—Debbie, Shona, John, Brian and kids.

Downy woodpecker

Backyard Ballet

From streams no oar hath rippled
And lakes that waft no sail,
From reaches vast and lonely
That know no hunter's trail,
The clamour of their calling
And the whistling of the flight
Fill all the day with marvel,
And with mystery, the night.[61]

Entertainment is the cream in our cappuccino: opera, ballet, hockey, snowmobiling, you name it. We moderns have out-Romaned the Romans in our pursuit of pleasure. Now, Mary Helen and I enjoy a concert as well as anyone and a recent production of the Nutcracker wowed us. But for sheer non-stop entertainment, our backyard ballet is hard to beat.

Saturday afternoon. I collapsed into my overstuffed chair in the den, levered my legs into the air, lifted my coffee cup and settled down to track the villain in a tale of espionage. But barely a paragraph into the plot, my eye caught movement out the back window. A gang of chickadees, their black caps bobbing, were hopping and skipping around the bird feeder.

A dive-bombing nuthatch scattered the chickadees to surrounding perches, where they choreographed their outrage in an intricate chickadee minuet. The white-breasted nuthatch hung upside down on the feeder and scanned her rivals with her cold orbs, daring any to contest her divine right to first pickings. Having laid down a circle of intimidation, she turned to the bird-bin with a vengeance. After scattering seed near and far, she rocketed away with a choice nugget in her beak. The chickadees swarmed back to take her place.

Below the feeder, juncos waltzed over the snow-covered ground, cleaning up after their wasteful chickadee cousins. The slate-coloured juncos, like the chickadees, travel in gregarious groups. But unlike the chickadees, they forage along the ground.

A shy tree sparrow adroitly de-husked seeds from the finch feeder a few feet away. Shortly, it was joined by a tolerant family of goldfinches who sedately settled on perches and munched away. Their quiet self-control contrasted sharply with the everlasting motion of the chickadees. How did they manage to de-husk the minute black Niger seeds with their ambidextrous beaks?

As I sat watching this backyard ballet, I was struck by the diverse personalities of the different species of birds. The nuthatch acted like a driven, high-power choleric, the chickadees like the fun-loving extroverts of birdland. The more sedate goldfinches were phlegmatic plodders and the junkos, gregarious but perfectionistic planners. The redpolls, however, seemed to be the nervous nellies of birdland.

A flock of twenty or thirty redpolls suddenly descended on the feeder, displacing the goldfinches. Acting like children fighting for space on a postage stamp ice rink, they crowded and jostled each other off the prime perches. Those excluded from the finch feeder floated to the ground, where they acted like a wild bunch of hockey players chasing a dozen pucks at once as they scrimmaged for the seeds scattered from above.

A few minutes later, a downy woodpecker, looking like the toy soldier in the Nutcracker, descended on the suet ball. He attacked the suet with a will. As I watched his antics, I wondered if the hairy woodpecker or the pileated would visit that day. Their precision drilling labels them as the technicians of birdland. They certainly know where to come for energy. Early in the winter we had heard a rat-a-tat-tat on the walls of the house. Peeking out through the window of our mud room, I spied a hairy woodpecker beating a tattoo on our log walls. That would not do! Deciphering the woodpecker code as outrage at my failure to hang up a suet ball, I quickly rectified the oversight—and they obliged by staying away from our walls.

The celebrated nature writer, R.D. Lawrence, drew great solace from the creatures inhabiting the woods near his cabin. Of the chickadees, he wrote:

> *I marvel at these perky little forest gymnasts, so delicate, yet tough enough to dare a Canadian winter. And so friendly, once they learn that man will not hurt them.*[62]

After patiently teaching them to feed from his hand Lawrence wrote:

> *There is something undefinably warming in the friendship of these little birds of my wilderness. It has a value beyond par and is almost impossible to describe for those who do not know the touch of something wild on their flesh. These are not the passive pets of man. They are primordial wildlings uncontaminated by captivity; minute, fragile things that have never known the confinement of a cage and their touch becomes a caress that carries*

with it the freedom of the wilderness. Wild and free are the birds; wild and free is the human upon whom they bestow their trust.[63]

While we have not felt their caress upon our hands, we do revel in their friendly chatter whenever we venture out to refill the feeder or bring in wood. And during the summer, we marvel at the hummingbirds who show no fear at our presence among the flowers they glean for nectar.

My ruminations were suddenly interrupted. All the birds exploded into the sky in a flurry of feathers. Perhaps they had caught the shadow of a circling hawk or spied a stalking cat. Silence descended. The curtain came down on Act II of that day's production of our backyard ballet—specially designed by the divine Choreographer. As Maltbie Babcock wrote in the hymn that is so popular;

> *This is my Father's world,*
> *and to my listening ears*
> *all nature sings,*
> *and round me rings*
> *the music of the spheres.*
> *…The birds their carols raise…*

Subtle, sweet melody! With a sigh of contentment and a little less enthusiasm for espionage, I returned to my book about spies among the gondolas of Venice.

Snowbound

Sharp is the frost, the Northern Light
Flickers and shoots his streamers bright;
Snow-drifts cumber the untracked road;
Bends the pine with its heavy load;
Each small star, though it shines so bright,
Looks half-pinched with the cold to-night.[64]

I was up early preparing for an editorial meeting in the city. With the coffee dripping, I turned to the wood stove. Stirring up the coals, I tossed on some kindling and soon had a blaze. I tried to make out the temperature on the thermometer outside the window, but it was still too dark and snow on the screen obscured my view. It was really chilly inside, too. While I waited impatiently for that first cup of coffee, I idly listened to the radio: "School is cancelled throughout Metro. Roselawn is open but no buses are running. Wait. I have a report from a cellular caller coming down Bayview. 'Bayview is terrible. Going maybe 5 kilometers an hour. I've seen a number of cars in the ditch.' Folks, we got hammered. The whole area. And it's still snowing. If you can stay home, do."

By this time I had grabbed my coat and turned on our outside lights. Stepping outside, I looked around. An unbroken blanket of snow covered everything. As I waded through foot deep snow, I could see that drifts covered our driveway. The road was hidden. It would be hours before the snowplows could clear the main arteries, let alone our country road.

I was going to miss the meeting. Taking Mary Helen a cup of coffee, I woke her up and broke the news. "Snow. Lots of snow!" A grin began to spread across my face. "Hallelujah, we're snowbound!"

Mary Helen grins her delight at being snowed in.

Sleepily, Mary Helen responded, "What, you've already been outside and without me?"

Mary Helen likes to wake up slowly with a cup of coffee in

her hands—but snow, that wakes her up quickly. I've never met anyone who becomes ecstatic over snow like she does. "Let's go outside!"

And so, as a dim light began to filter through the falling snow, we bundled up and stepped outside. We could make out rabbit tracks going along the wall under the eaves. We plowed up the driveway and out onto the road. The neighbour's four-wheel drive pick-up had obviously been past. Like little kids at Disneyworld, we leapfrogged through the driving snow, until we came to the open field with its view of the valley. The wind threw streamers of snow at our faces as we tried to make out Cupcake Hill. Invisible. The chill soon turned us around.

Back inside our snug home, we poured some more coffee and curled up in our favourite chairs. Picking up the weekend newspaper I couldn't help but let out a long sigh. After a busy couple of weeks and a heavy schedule on Sunday, we were pooped. How wonderful to have an unscheduled day off! "Providence is so much kinder to us than we are to ourselves," I murmured.

We spent a leisurely day. I picked up a book that I'd abandoned before Christmas. From time to time, we shared choice passages or inspirational nuggets from our readings. Often, however, we were distracted by the action outside. Chickadees and nuthatches, song sparrows and juncos came looking for food. Our downy woodpecker returned again and again to the suet bag for nourishment. Blue jays flew in and out. With snow covering forage areas, several new birds arrived. As I fed the fire, I was thankful I'd been able to get a good supply of wood into the mud-room before the storm hit.

Occasionally, we ventured outside to work at clearing the driveway. At that time we didn't have a snowblower. By late afternoon, the snowplow had cleared one lane along the road and a distant hum from the north beckoned us to explore.

Topping a rise, we could make out the winking lights of snowmobiles on the snow highway a mile north of our house. Attracted by the fresh snow, executives all over the area had called in sick and cranked up their machines. Many offices in Toronto were short-staffed that week. Sno-108, a winter snowmobile highway stretching east to west through our area links up with 49,000 kilometres of groomed trails throughout Ontario. Enthusiasts estimate there are 175,000 active snowmobilers in the province who participate in 280 individual clubs. Each club takes responsibility to groom one section of the largest network of trails in the world.

We paused under a snow-draped pine to watch the action. An almost steady stream of machines raced by us. Ski-doos, Arctic Cats, Hondas, Polaris; machines that cost thousands of dollars. Red. White. Florescent Green. Black. Many of today's machines have seat-warmers. Some drivers communicate back and forth through headsets. A few trailed sleds full of waving kids. Helmeted, goggled, snowmobile-suit clad riders giddy with the abundance of snow—not too common in southern Ontario—waved at us wildly as they sped by.

A longing for quiet and relief from the acrid fumes, soon sent us back home Most of the day found us curled up with a favourite book. And of course—in our warm and cheery home under its blanket of snow—romance soon blossomed. We can never figure out why people don't like to be snowbound!

Red Flag Flu

Sir, more than kisses,
Letters mingle souls;
For, thus friends absent speak.[65]

February is a month of promises broken, hopes dashed. Ice one day, slush the next. Tracers of drifting snow in the morning, cold rain by afternoon. In the mall people wheeze and cough and hack and blow. At home I catch Red Flag Flu. Bad.

At this time of year, mornings find me listening more carefully than usual. I keep looking at my watch. Periodically, I abandon my work to prowl about the house. When I hear Sandy's car stop on the road, I jog to the window to see if the mail has arrived. Although endemic, my touch of Red Flag Flu is more pronounced in February.

This particular malady only strikes those country dwellers who still have rural mail delivery. Entrepreneurs who work out of their homes contract particularly bad cases of this flu. In my own instance, I find it hard to concentrate until the red flag on the mailbox signals the arrival of mail. I try to keep my optimism in check—could it be a letter from New Zealand, a card from a friend, a cheque from a publisher? Instead I discover bills and junk mail, again!

In the country, mail is part of the rhythm of life. At the centre of that cadence, Sandy—our postie—remains consistently cheerful and friendly. Her inevitable smile confirms what she says: "I love it. Every day is different. And I just love being out in the fresh air and sunshine."

Sandy is responsible to deliver over 3000 pieces of mail a day to 500 rural customers on a 120-kilometre circuit. Every day she reports to the Post Office in Port Hope at 7:00 a.m. to sort her mail. Depending on volume, this takes her two or more hours. When I asked her about it, she commented, "People in this area get a lot of mail. More than folks in town."

Actually delivering the mail takes, at the very least, three-and-a-half hours, usually more. So, by 1:30 on Monday, a heavy mail day, our red flag is usually signaling "mail." As the week progresses and the volume of mail decreases, Sandy delivers the mail earlier. I have the time gauged quite accurately; 12:00 on Tuesday, 11:30 on Wednesday, 11:00 on Thursday, and about 10:30 on Fridays, depending on whether or not she has a lot of advertising flyers to add to the mail.

Monday to Friday, whether it sleets, snows, hails, or shines bright and warm, Sandy's little red car criss-crosses the concessions. During the last four years, she failed to finish mail delivery only three times. In each case, ice storms were the culprit. Ice so bad she couldn't stand up on it. Ice so slippery her car slid sideways down the road before she called off her attempts to reach all the mailboxes.

Only extremely bad weather aborts mail delivery. She explained, "We are warned that failure to deliver mail will instantly result in our contract being cancelled. Each of us have to train a back-up who will take over immediately if we become sick."

"Do you have holidays?"

"I had one day last year. Two years ago, my back-up took it for a week. But I do get the weekends and regular holidays like Thanksgiving and Christmas off."

I was amazed at her delivery record, given the extreme weather we have had during the past few years: snowstorms, hail, weeks of rain turning back roads into swamps, fog. "There's one two-kilometre stretch back into the woods for two mail-boxes that I hate," she exclaimed. "It's murder if the weather is bad. It's really hard on cars. Mufflers, shocks, front end. When we have a lot of rain, like we have recently, pot-holes develop overnight. I know every regular pot-hole, but rain creates new ones. Fortunately, my husband Jim is handy with cars."

Sandy not only loves her job, but people and dogs too. "If Fen sees me, he won't go back home until I pet him." Fen is an Irish wolfhound that stands as tall as her car. "I'm a sucker for dogs. I pet them... except for the Rottweilers and Boxers. I don't go near them."

Rural mail delivery reflects the community spirit common in the country. People actually know their neighbours. Along city streets, anonymous houses line the avenues identified only by numbers; 162 Smith Street or 10365 Wilmot Road. Out here in the country, every mailbox is a social ice-breaker. Even if we haven't met the new neighbours to the north yet, we know their name. It's on their mailbox. Country homes and farms are not anonymous brick or wood boxes. They have a recognizable identity. There's the Becker farm and the Hosteter place.

"The fun part is remembering who's living with who and whose kids belong to who," Sandy commented. With so many people failing to update their addresses, she has to work hard to keep up with people along the 120 kilometres of concessions she travels. This is especially difficult with new people who move in without an address notice being posted or people with the same names. "There are five C. Wilsons. A lot of Mercers. A bunch of J. Toms. Then the kids start getting their own mail! Who has been divorced, who has died, who has gotten married? If a letter arrives with a strange name, I hold it a day and ask around. I usually find out where they live!"

We marvel at her ability to keep up with comings and goings. Three of our neighbours have moved in the last two years, yet she is unerring in her delivery. In spite of the fact that there are a lot of Wrights in the community, we have received mail from New Zealand with no more address than Grandma & Grandpa Wright, Campbellcroft. And we've received lots of mail with the wrong address. This kind of commitment means the "Addressee Unknown—Return to Sender" stamp gets little use here.

We don't take mail delivery for granted. We know bureaucrats in Ottawa have no concept of its importance to the rural psyche. To cut costs, they keep putting up more of those multi-person, mega-mailboxes that require people drive to a central location to collect their mail. They have no idea of the benefits to the mental health of millions that accrue from rural mail delivery. With all their predictions about mushrooming medical costs to care for aging baby boomers, they ought to recognize the health benefits to society from all those daily jogs along maple lined laneways, past snowy fields, to the mailbox.

Sandy faces her daily share of mailbox drama. "Starlings are a problem. They love to make their nests in mailboxes. I've opened a box and had one of them fly in my face. One customer turns her mailbox around every year to let me know there is a nest in it. Until nesting season is over, I have to put her mail in the newspaper box. Then there are bees that make their hives in the boxes... and earwigs. I hate earwigs."

Rural mailboxes not only identify, they entertain. Neighbours up and down the concessions express their personality and

creativity through their mailboxes: some resemble tractors, some barns, log cabins, cows, horses, geese, cardinals. Ours is a loon.

Most important, the red flag on our mailbox signals letters! Some letters are from distant friends. Since Providence took us around the world, we have friends in many ports: Australia, Paraguay, Pakistan, India, Ecuador, Philippines, Ireland, and, of course, many states of the U.S. Until e-mail began to speed up communication, letters—even form letters—kept us up on who had a baby, who had moved where, who had retired, who had surgery. There are few things are as satisfying as receiving a missive from an old friend.

Much more could be said about rural mail delivery and Sandy, our intrepid postie who waves whenever she sees us, but it's that time of day. I've got to run. I just heard her car. She may have delivered a letter with a huge advance from some New York publisher or a card from Australia.

> *Make new friends, but keep the old;*
> *Those are silver, these are gold.*
> *New-made friendship, like new wine,*
> *Age will mellow and refine.*
> *Friendships that have stood the test—*
> *Time and change—are surely best;*
> *Brow may wrinkle, hair grow gray;*
> *Friendship never know decay.*
> *For 'mid old friends, tried and true,*
> *Once more we our youth renew.*
> *But old friends, alas! may die;*
> *New friends must their place supply.*
> *Cherish friendship in your breast—*
> *New is good, but old is best;*
> *Make new friends, but keep the old;*
> *Those are silver, these are gold.*[66]

SPRING

Floating Down the Ganny

Now hath a wonder lit the saddened eyes
Long misted by a grievous winter clime;
And now the dull heart leaps with love's surprise
And sings its joy. For tis the happy time,
And all the brooding earth is full of chime,
And all the hosts of sleepers underground
Have burst out suddenly in glorious prime;
And all the airy spirits now have found
Their wonted shrines with life and love entwined 'round.[67]

A television crew waited to interview a slim blonde in a black wet suit as she waded ashore from a raft made of giant inner tubes. Her face and hands were red from the cold. Extending a mike toward her, a crewman in a warm ski jacket asked, "How many years have you been entering the Ganny race?"

"Five," she replied as she stretched to rescue a paddle floating by.

"Why do you do it?" he queried.

"I'm crazy," she answered with a shiver and cockeyed grin. She turned away to join her crew in hoisting their weird craft onto their shoulders for the run to the finish line in the centre of town.

Three hundred and fifty odd participants had joined her in plunking down good money to enter the annual "Float Your Fanny Down the Ganny" race. This strange local ritual harks back to 1980, the year the placid Ganaraska River swelled over its banks to flood downtown Port Hope. As the town returned to normal, they decided to do something to commemorate their suffering. But instead of commissioning a dirge, they created a celebration.

Crazy craft on the Ganaraska River

What started out as a local catharsis for the winter blahs now draws fully a third of its contestants from outside the area—some from the United States. This is no warm water, summertime romp. It's traditionally the first week in April and the Ganaraska River is swollen with frigid water from snow and ice melting in the Northumberland Hills. Overhead, a stiff north wind usually blows leaden clouds over a grey landscape. Temperatures often hover between five and ten degrees Celsius.

The opportunity to see mad mariners brave bone-chilling water in a slapstick attempt to bid winter goodbye brought spectators from far and near. At every road crossing along the Ganny north of Port Hope, spectators lined the bridges. A huge crowd gathered at Corbett's dam, where participants would portage. In the centre of town thousands more thronged the riverbank. Many brought lawn chairs, picnic coolers and thermoses of coffee. The crowd spanned the generations. Old timers joked with teens. Parents pushed baby strollers. Family groups reclined on blankets. Dogs of every description raced through the crowd.

Laughing, gesturing, eating, drinking—people celebrating the end of winter buried the gloomy memories of the great flood that started it all. Hot dog vendors barked their wares. Guides sold cookies. A line snaked up the hill to a steam-belching french fry wagon. Cars choked the town for a mile around. The nearby United Church advertised a Ganny Craft Sale and Hot Lunch.

Forty feet up, in a cherry picker that extended out over the river, sat the MC in top hat and tux. He tapped his mike to get attention. "Folks, I think that's the local police rounding the bend. Uh, oh, they've got trouble. Their raft's comin' apart. Hey that's Jerry trying to grab the runaway barrel. To serve and protect? I don't know about their competence, folks. If they can't build a raft that stays together how can they protect us? Hold on folks, Jerry's got the barrel but is he going to be swept under the rope?… No, he's got it! But there goes his paddle. Well, let's give 'em a hand—they look pretty wet and miserable."

Two ropes stretched across the rapids in the middle of town, a quarter mile upstream from where the river empties into Lake Ontario. When participants are swept past the landing stage, they can grab the ropes and hang on until local firefighters reel them in. As I watched, some did tumble by beyond the reach of their rescuers, only to beach in the shallow water farther down.

First aid workers with the St. John Ambulance organization waited near the landing stage. Both an ambulance and a fire and rescue vehicle were also parked beside the cherry picker. Some contestants shivered around a log fire blazing off to one side. Ominous! Rescue personnel, however, act more as insurance than anything. No one gets badly hurt.

The race began at a conservation area nine kilometers upriver. It was run in two stages. Canoeists and kayakers set out at 10:00 a.m. When they reached the landing area in Port Hope, they had to bodily lift their boats out of the water and run with them to the finish line in the centre of town. The main street soon looked like a scene from a disaster movie.

At 11:00, the crazy crafts took to the water. They came in every shape and size. Two inner tubes with plywood decks drifted by to the cheers of the crowd. The lone navigator on the first deck wore multi-coloured pants and a hat decorated with plastic fruit. Trailing behind him on a second inner tube, his Labrador—wearing a dress, sat serenely surveying the crowds. A few minutes behind them, a strange craft flying the American flag floated by. Their raft was fabricated from steel barrels and inner tubes. The five men on board wore a motley assortment of wetsuits, clothing, and life jackets. They paddled as fast as they could to catch up with four men in an even stranger dugout wearing—I couldn't believe it—short-sleeved T-shirts! As they neared their target, the Yankees doused them with their wildly splashing paddles.

Three plywood rafts on huge inner tubes tied together drifted sideways across the river, as their crews desperately tried to avoid capsizing. They were quickly drenched by the crew on another raft made of a hodge-podge of styrofoam and inner tubes. Their victims, abandoning any attempt to steer, rose to retaliate with giant water pistols.

A raft made completely of sealed tubes of aluminum next

came into view. Stable but not buoyant! Its crew tried vainly to control the craft while they sat submerged a foot below the surface. They looked like a mini-sub surfacing for repairs. Just then a raft of cedar poles crewed by a wild group of howling men and women lumbered by. Another crew, seated in regal splendour on white plastic chairs, suddenly capsized, dumping everyone in the drink. Paddles, chairs, bits of lumber, styrofoam, inner tubes and hats floated away.

Many of the men and women who took part wore wet suits to ward off the chill. A considerable number, however, made do with rubber boots, galoshes, blue jeans, and raincoats. All of them arrived drenched. Their faces were red and their hands were raw after fighting each other and the current, and lugging their contraptions around Corbett's Dam. Some even substituted snow shovels or brooms for paddles. Through it all, the spectators hooted and cheered and laughed and nudged each other while they drank coffee and scarfed up dogs.

Walton Street was thronged with people. The line of parents waiting for their kids to ride the elephant was half a block long. Others tasted samples from the Chili Cook-off, voting for the best chili in the county. A husband and wife team serenaded the crowds with their violin and guitar. A clown shaped like an English cucumber with stars painted on his face made balloon animals for the kids. At the main intersection canoes and crazy craft surrounded a flat bed truck with a speaker system belting out country music, comments and announcements about the day's events.

It's spring fever, Ganaraska style. It's April foolishness. Just the kind of craziness to banish the winter blahs. But don't ask me to climb into one of those contraptions.

Make me over, Mother April,
When the sap begins to stir!

Make me man or make me woman,
Make me oaf or ape or human,
Cup of flower or cone of fir:
Make me anything but neuter
When the sap begins to stir! [68]

The Taste of Spring

Hail to the pride of the forest, hail
To the maple tall and green,
It yields a treasure which never shall fail
While leaves on its boughs are seen.
When the snows of winter are melting fast,
And the sap begins to rise,
And the biting breath of the frozen blast
Yields to the spring's soft sighs.[69]

"Sap's running!" came the cry from the sugar bush, where hundreds of gaunt, fissured old maples stood like scarred warriors hooked up to intravenous tubes. Drifts of snow still blanketed the ground beneath them. The nights were frigid but during the day the sun had begun to warm the tracery of branches supplicating the sky.

Sweet sap from the sugar maples in Matt's 20-acre sugar bush had begun to trickle through the miles of black tubing to the great evaporator where Matt and his youngest son Jeremy

stoked the fire. His oldest son, John, checked out the new-fan-
gled osmosis machine that would extract half the water from the
sap. His wife, Helen, lined up the stock of bottles, tins, and
labels they would need to sell the syrup to the hordes who would
soon descend. Clouds of fragrant steam began to envelop the
hut, and ever so slowly, watery sap was mysteriously converted
into maple syrup, the elixir of spring!

With the first break in the weather, Matt and his family had
been hard at work patrolling the bush. They had checked every
inch of the miles of tubing linking the trees to the giant reservoir where the sap was to be collected. Every puncture had been
repaired where mice or squirrels, chipmunks or raccoons had
gnawed through the tubing to get at the sweet residue from the
previous year. The vacuum pump used to create suction on the
tubing system had been tested and was ready.

Word spread quickly. From nearby schools and distant condos, people came in droves to taste spring's potion. With our
grandchildren in tow we joined them. Before visiting the sugar
shack we climbed aboard a sleigh pulled by two giant Percherons
for a tour of a section that had been set aside to demonstrate
how pioneers prepared maple syrup. The tails of the gentle
giants were braided and decorated with bows. Joel, the driver,
was dressed like a Quebec habitant. Sleigh bells rang as we clop-
clopped through the still crisp snow past trees festooned with
pails to collect the sap.

At the far end of the circuit everyone got off the sleigh in a
clearing. In the centre a great black cast-iron pot boiled away
over an open fire. Dressed in a pioneer costume, Matt's oldest
son John sauntered into the clearing carrying two wooden pails
hanging from a yoke on his shoulder. After emptying the pails
into a barrel near the fire, he proceeded to feed the fire and stir
the pot. Then he invited us to have a seat on one of the bench-

es around the fire while he told us the legend of Manabush.

John explained that long before European explorers came to Canada, the native peoples learned how to draw off maple sap and boil it to make sugar. They showed French settlers the process. The practice became so much a part of colony life in the 17th and 18th centuries that syrup developed into a major source of pure sugar.

He continued, "As legend has it, Nokomis (the land) was the first to pierce the maple tree trunk in an attempt to collect sugar water. Later Manabush discovered that this maple sugar water (syrup) was ready to eat. While she found it delicious, she was concerned.

"She went to her grandmother and said, 'Grammy, it isn't good that trees produce sugar so easily; because man may become lazy if maple trees produce sugar with so little effort. We must find a way to make them work. Before we can enjoy this fine nectar, it would be good that men be forced to chop wood and pass the night watching over the boiling.'

"Since her grandmother, Nokomis, seemed indifferent to her pleas, Manabush determined to prevent men from becoming lazy. To do so, she climbed to the top of a maple tree with a bucket full of water. She then poured the water into the centre of the tree, thereby dissolving the sugar within the trunk. Since then, sugar water is no longer syrup but sap with only 1 to 2 percent pure sugars. And so, we have to work really hard to enjoy maple syrup. It takes 30 gallons of maple sap to make 1 gallon of syrup. Take a few minutes to wander around," he concluded.[70]

Lifting the protecting lid on one sap bucket, Shareena peered inside. "It looks just like water," she exclaimed.

"That's why they keep the fire burning in the sugar shack," Adrianna explained knowingly as she stuck out her finger to catch a drop forming on the spigot. "It's sweet!" she blurted.

"Let me see," pleaded Kassandra looking up at the sap bucket from below. I lifted her up to peer inside and taste a drop or two on her finger.

On the way back I plied Joel, the driver of the sleigh, with questions about the trees. "We have to choose the trees with care," he explained, "or the taps can stunt their growth. We bypass all trees under 25 cm in diameter. In mature trees we bore holes 5 cm deep with a drill and drive in spigots on which we hang the pails or link up with the network of tubing. See over there? Some trees have as many as three taps. In a good year, each tap can produce two pounds or more of maple syrup. The weather is a big factor. If it stays below freezing, the sap stops running. If it warms up too much, the quality of the sap deteriorates."

Part way back, Joel let Shareena, oldest of the three, help hold the reins. The other two, resentful of the privilege bestowed upon their older sister, pleaded for turns to no avail. But as the sugar shack came in sight, they soon forgot their indignation.

Like bees at a barbecue, a throng of children surrounded a long trough. The trough was packed with snow on which Jeremy had poured streams of pure maple syrup. On the cold snow the syrup quickly congealed into toffee-like strands. The children were busy winding it around Popsicle sticks, which they popped into their mouths. Our gang jumped off the sleigh to join them. "Don't have too much," I urged. "We've got a breakfast of pancakes coming up."

With great difficulty, we tore them away from the toffee trough. Their hands were sticky. In fact, they seemed sticky all over! Adrianna had a gob of syrup in her hair and Kassandra had it on her mittens. After wiping off the worst, we joined the line of people going through the sugar shack.

At one end stood an enormous tank full of sap collected through the network of tubing. It fed a modern innovation, a reverse osmosis machine that removed half the water. From the osmosis machine the sap entered one end of an evaporator. The evaporator was a series of connected stainless steel cooking pans heated by the fire below. As the sap boiled, more was added from the tank, creating a flow through the pans. Clouds of steam rose as the sap became more concentrated. By the time it reached the end of the evaporator, its colour had changed to a light amber.

Matt explained the process. "The art of sugaring is centred here on the evaporator. We have to monitor the depth of the sap and adjust the feed tank valve to keep it constant. The heat has to be kept just right, or the sap will boil over and scorch the pans —ruining a whole batch. Down at this end we keep skimming off the foam. But most important, we have to monitor the density of the sap in the final pans, the finishing pans, and draw it off at the exact right time. See the thermometer?"

Dipping in a ladle, he poured some out. "Just right," he remarked, turning to his wife Marie, who was already beginning to drain off the concentrated syrup.

Our granddaughters were a little bored by the lengthy explanation. "When are we gonna have pancakes?" Kassandra asked rather plaintively.

"Right now," Mary Helen replied, as we headed out of the sugar shack in search of flapjacks.

Beside the shack, a covered shed was filled with picnic tables. At one end, several of Matt's daughters (I wondered if you needed a big family to run a sugar operation!) cooked a continuous stream of pancakes and sausages. Soon we were hard at work, scoffing sausages and piles of pancakes slathered with all the maple syrup you could eat. Ah, the marvelous taste of a Canadian spring! In a sawdust-sprinkled space in front of the flapjack shed, three fiddlers serenaded us with Celtic melodies as we ate. Then four sets of square dancers in period costumes began to kick up the sawdust as they danced to the screaming fiddles.

On our way home, the kids all talked at once. "I loved the toffee best," exclaimed Kassandra.

"An' the horsies," broke in Adrianna. "The driver let me pet one."

"I'm going to write a story about the pioneers making maple syrup," said Shareena.

"An I'm going to draw a picture," rejoined Adrianna."

"Well, I'm going to make maple syrup muffins," said Mary Helen, as she waved the recipe she had picked up in the souvenir shop. "Can we have some?" we all chimed in unison.

Sap is boiling,
Skies are clear,
Maple syrup
Time is here.[71]

Techno-robin

The trees to their innermost marrow
Are touched by the sun;
The robin is here and the sparrow:
Spring is begun!

The sleep and the silence are over:
These petals that rise
Are the eyelids of earth that uncover
Her numberless eyes.[72]

O fficially, spring was still two days off when we heard the spring serenade—a robin song. The heralds of spring had returned! Like two fat friars singing vespers, our resident robins warbled their ode to a warming sun before waddling along the verge in search of lunch.

Tentacles of dingy snow still reached out in an expiring effort to strangle the wakening lawn. Here and there, a daffodil had extended a green finger to test the frosty air. Not so cautious, crocus and snowdrops bravely challenged the retreating snow. Almost under a snowbank, a Johnny jump-up raised its smiling face to the wan sun.

Sub-zero nights dispelled any wistful thoughts of an early spring. And in a convulsion of wrath, winter unleashed a day-long snow storm. But in some mysterious way our robins endured winter's last gasp. Somehow, they knew that spring was on the threshold. And on the third day after their return, the sun banished the snow and unveiled the lawn.

The sight of the first robins meant more—much more, to us than the vaunted return of the swallows to Capistrano. We knew winter was in full retreat. Oh, there would be a few more skirmishes, but Robin and Robinette assured us that winter was beaten with much more certainty than the forecasters.

Euphoria lasted almost a week. By then, our spring heralds had mutated into techno-robins. They're never content to make their nest in the big juniper by the front door like their fore-bears. Not for them a traditional spot in one of the oaks. No, they believe in upward mobility.

One day, on our way out for groceries, we looked around in bewilderment at the bits of grass and dirt on the car inside the garage. Looking up, we spied grass and string hanging down from the garage door opener above us. The robins were building a condo on our garage door opener!

They had chosen a perfect spot—for them. Safe from neighbouring cats. Warm and dry. But we couldn't have them jamming the door open for the rest of the summer. Hardening our hearts, we braved an unmerciful scolding to remove their unfinished nest.

The battle over the garage continued for weeks. "Is the garage door shut?" we asked each other periodically throughout the day. Since we usually leave the door open during the daytime, we had to program ourselves to adopt a new pattern lest Robin and Robinette return to their building project.

Obviously displeased, they turned their attentions to our car. When we parked it outside, they perched on the side mirrors to preen. But with preening came besmirching the sides of the car with robin poop. What a mess! Now, we had to remind ourselves to park the car inside the garage and keep the door closed.

Sundays usually found us in a rush—and forgetful of our winged protagonists. Running late for church, and wearing our Sunday best, we dashed out to car—only to find each door hideously smeared. What to do? Race off to church to park our sullied chariot in the midst of all those spotless cars, cars lovingly washed and polished on Saturday? We couldn't face the social ostracism. There was nothing else to do but grab the hose and risk soaking our Sunday suits while we cleaned off the robin mess. Perhaps you fail to empathize with our worry about being late for church. But then again, you may not be the one leading the service! As we accelerated out the driveway, we heard two robins chortle in triumph behind us.

Our resident robins seemed obsessed with mirrors and windows. In the early morning, when I settled into my favourite chair to enjoy the country quietness, I heard strange sounds coming from the living room. Peering in, I spied Robin prancing up and down in front of the sliding glass door to the deck. Like some feathered Don Quixote, he pecked wildly at the window. Then he flew to the deck railing. Cocking his head to one side he glanced back at the glass and launched another furious attack on the glass. The duel continued for a month. Spring hormones had pushed Robin over the edge.

After weeks of reminding each other to be sure the car was in the garage and the door closed, we appeared to have won the battle. Where could Robin and Robinette have gone? The wishing well? The thicket by the road? The ancient birch? Nothing so prosaic. When I went to fetch our ladder for some postponed outdoor maintenance, I discovered their nest on top of the ladder! I had hung the ladder horizontally on the outside garage wall, high up under the eaves, where it would be inconspicuous to the break-and-enter crowd. Obviously it was not inconspicuous to our exploring robins. After extensive research they declared it the perfect site for their brood. Admitting defeat— and having a genuine excuse, I postponed repairs and allowed them to raise their young. But why an aluminum ladder? Why not a high tree? Had they added to their preference for high tech gadgets and mirrors an affinity for extruded metal?

Now, we loved Robin and Robinette, but we were not quite ready to cede our property to their hegemony. These are not gregarious chickadees or shy nuthatches willing to acknowledge our superiority. Our robins scolded us whenever we stepped onto their field of worms, what we had mistakenly thought was our lawn!

The following year, we carefully kept the garage door down during the spring. And we tried to remember to park the car inside. We hid the ladder. But Robin and Robinette's love affair with modernity was not to be denied. After Master Robin's spring joust with our sliding doors, he wed Mrs. Robin and they set up residence on top of our motion lights! We admired their choice. This too was safe from cruising hawks, high and dry under the eaves—though hardly tidy. It was downright annoying. They knocked one light cockeyed with their comings and goings and dripped mud and straw down the wall. However, they won again. That summer, we yielded the use of our motion lights. I wonder what next year will bring?

Green against the draggled drift,
Faint and frail and first,
Buy my northern bloodroot

And I'll know where you were nursed!
Robin down the logging road whistles,
"Come to me!"
Spring has found the maple-grove, the sap is running free,
All the winds of Canada call the ploughing rain.
Take the flower and turn the hour,
and kiss your love again![73]

Eric's Folly

There are pleasures you cannot buy,
Treasures you cannot sell,
And not the smallest of these
Is the gift and glory of trees.[74]

I t was still early spring and Mary Helen, as usual, had begun to wonder about my disappearances.

When I slipped inside after one of my jaunts, she queried, "Where have you been, honey?"

"Oh, just out," I replied innocently.

"Doing what?" she persisted, with that endearing lift of her eyebrows.

"Nothing really. I picked up a few seedlings, that's all." Actually, I finagled 300 white pine, spruce, cedar, larch and oak seedlings from the conservation officer. A gold mine!

I guess it's a kind of spring fever. I had slipped away to the nearby conservation centre to beg or buy any tree seedlings they have left over from large orders. I had also visited a roadside gash to rescue some cedar and maple from an approaching road crew. I arrived home with my booty, put it carefully away in the garage and slunk into the house with a guilty smirk.

"More trees!" she expostulated, "When will you have time to put them in? Have you forgotten? You go away tomorrow for two days, then you have that meeting on Saturday. What about your preparation for Sunday?"

"Don't worry, I'll find the time."

Two days later, I returned home just in time for supper. After a gobbled meal, I raced outside to plant treasure. With one eye on the fading light I grubbed holes as fast as I could in the tangled grasses and poison ivy at one end of our property. Before darkness descended I'd put sixty or so seedlings to bed in the slumbering earth.

Saturday saw me up early digging holes beneath the scrubby Manitoba Maples for some oak seedlings. Later, after returning from a meeting, I planted a few larch and spruce. By stealing time from this and that, I was able to complete the planting by the middle of the following week. Although a few seedlings looked bedraggled, I felt confident that most would survive. Later on, I added several maples and beech that I rescued from a roadside slated to be bulldozed.

Every spring Mary Helen and I spar over priorities. She worries about spring cleaning, all the things that need fixing, and the appalling mess left by the woodpile at the back door. My mind, however, is on more pressing priorities.

On the phone, Mary Helen reported my exploits to our daughter. "Debbie, you won't believe what your dad is up to. He's planted another 300 trees." Talking to friends in Toronto, she pretended exasperation; "You know Eric. He's been out there in the dark planting hundreds of trees. We must have thousands by now."

I don't mind her gentle ribbing. She may tease me about "Eric's folly," but in reality, Mary Helen loves trees as much as I. She's just not as keen about neglecting spring cleaning to plant them while they are still dormant. But I've got Martin Luther on my side! When asked why he put so much effort into tree planting when the Lord might return and call the world to judgement, he replied, "Even if I knew the world would end tomorrow, I would continue to plant my trees."

My muscles ached, my to-do list was longer than ever, but my soul was singing. Already hundreds of red and white pine, white cedar and spruce, black walnut and white ash planted in other years had fought their way through the underbrush. Here and there Jack pine, birch, beech, red oak, and ironwood enriched the woodland mosaic I was striving to create. I'd even added a few exotics; Austrian pine, Norway spruce, Colorado blue spruce, and mountain ash.

We own a wedge of property about one and three quarter acres in size. Half is in grass and garden. Until we came, the remainder was a tangle of underbrush. There was a twisted old willow, a giant white birch, two great oaks, several red maples, a scattering of black cherries, and a few Scotch pines. What the Manitoba maple didn't choke out were smothered by poison ivy and sumac. A lone white pine, my favourite tree, guarded the ridge. Fortunately our property was enhanced by a goodly stand of red and white pine gracing neighbouring land.

Very early, a vision took shape, the dream of a mixed forest with at least one of every tree native to Ontario. Even before I studied forestry, I loved the woodlands. I always longed for a place where I could celebrate our forest diversity, a place where I could nurture trees to be enjoyed by our great grandchildren.

I could see it in my mind: our log home embraced on three sides by a wealth of textures and shapes tinted with a hundred subtle shades of green; our wedge of sandy nothingness become a natural arboretum; a tree-house nestling in the oak behind the house; a swing hanging from a two-foot thick black cherry; our grandchildren leading their children along a path weaving through the property. I can see them pointing out the different trees—dozens of varieties of evergreens, scores of hardwoods. "Your great grandpa planted that beech in '98 and that larch the same year."

I can dream, can't I? Even if we have to sell and move away, someone will enjoy the trees we planted—and I will have struck a blow for ecological equilibrium. Our home nestles against the 10,500 acre Ganaraska Forest. Government cutbacks put unrelenting pressure on this non-profit conservatory to sell off pieces of land to meet expenses. All over Canada, the snarl of advancing chainsaws is forcing more and more conservation authorities to retreat. And yet, we all profit by the lyrical green spaces that grace our countryside.

Canadians have been caricatured too long as loggers and miners. In 1855, Sir Edmund W. Head, then governor general noted, "You Canadians have a prejudice against trees."[75] Two decades earlier, Catharine Parr Traill had written, "They would not spare the ancient oak from feelings of veneration, nor look with regard for any thing but its use as timber."[76] A contemporary, Anna Jameson, wrote, "A Canadian settler hates a tree, regards it as his natural enemy, as something to be destroyed, eradicated, annihilated by all and any means."[77]

The great stump fences that line Trespass Road, not far from our home, bear mute testimony to the truth of their lament. They are the meagre skeletons of the vast forests that clothed the Northumberland Hills. Unbridled cutting turned this section of the Oak Ridges Moraine, one of southern Ontario's great aquifers, into an eroded wasteland only rescued by massive reforestation. Fortunately, across the country, public interest in ecology is on the rise.

Danger, however, still lurks. As I will describe later, even here along our quiet road, mankind's manic lust to witness the crash of forest giants would result in an orgy of destruction. But that story must wait for a later chapter.

> *We stand beneath the pines and enter*
> *the grand pillared aisles*
> *with a feeling of mute reverence;*
> *these stately trunks bearing their plumed head*
> *so high above us*
> *seem a meet roofing for His temple*
> *who reared them to His praise.*[78]

Bloodroot—among the earliest of the spring flowers

Wildflower Week

For winter's rains and ruins are over,
And all the season of snows and sins;
The days dividing lover and lover,
The light that loses, the night that wins;
And time remembered is grief forgotten,
And frosts are slain and flowers begotten,
And in green underwood and cover
Blossom by blossom the spring begins.[79]

Our mad motorcyclist shattered the country quiet with the thunder of his exhaust. Oblivious to spring beauties blooming along his path, he thundered through the woodlands. Ar-h-h-roa-r-rs echoed from the waking ridges. He threw himself at the steepest parts of the hill below us. I caught a glimpse of his red helmet as he rocketed over the crest scattering gravel to the four winds. Scars on the path and a flung beer-can marked his passing.

We now had an answer to our spring ditty; "Spring has sprung. The grass is riz. I wonder where the motorcyclist is?"

Dirt bike jockeys were not alone in feeling the stir of hormones. Our phone and fax went berserk. I was informed about a deadline that could not be postponed, an editorial meeting that couldn't be delayed, and a convention I had to attend. After cruising through winter in low gear, semi-hibernating Canadians feel an adrenaline rush. Why? Is it the thought of the approaching summer? Perhaps they realize that in order to enjoy the lazy, hazy days ahead, they have to race through a catch-up spring. But why can't people schedule conventions in February and meetings in March? Don't they realize that spring is wildflower time?

> *She comes with gusts of laughter,*
> *The music as of rills;*
> *With tenderness and sweetness,*
> *The wisdom of the hills.* [80]

Delicate brush strokes of spring green had begun to touch the dead fields and naked trees. Flowery pendants hung from aspens and soft maples. Rainbow trout fought their way up the Ganaraska to hurl themselves at the fish ladder. A rose-breasted grosbeak visited our feeder. Robin and Robinette ferried straw to their secret nest. All the signs pointed to wildflower week. The time had come to cancel appointments and head outdoors.

Wildflowers began to peek through the warming humus in a race to flower before the forest canopy closed out the warming sun. Bloodroot was the first to unfold white petals. Soon after, clusters of delicate spring beauties and then pink and white hepaticas fringed the forest pathways. Shortly, dog-toothed violets carpeted the rich soil below the maples with blades of spotted green before they gathered strength to unveil their shy saffron flowers.

Society seemed determined to distract us from this spring pageant. Marketing types turned up the pressure. Merchandising flyers overflowed our mailbox. Malls planned massive sales. Real Estate agents moved into high gear.

The house needed spring cleaning. The lawn cried out for attention—rolling and aerating and fertilizing and cutting. The flower beds beckoned accusingly whenever I glanced out the window. A flood of frantic activity engulfed us just when we ought to have been taking a break to walk in our woodlands.

Every year we tell ourselves, "Next year we'll make sure we take time for an unhurried stroll through a fairyland of nodding trilliums." And every year the demands make mincemeat of our firmest resolve.

The woodland wildflowers that carpet our hardwood forests in the spring, bloom only during the narrow window of time after the warming sun brings them to life and before the overarching trees throw out a leafy curtain blocking that selfsame sun. We have, perhaps, two weeks to enjoy one of God's greatest displays. The timing will vary from year to year, depending on the weather. It could be really early, an El Niño spring in late April, or a delayed spring extending into mid-May.

Whenever it comes, we should call a halt to our madness and declare one whole week, "Wildflower Week!" Then everyone could take a holiday from work and shopping to walk the woodland trails. The experience might change our whole national psyche! Natural beauty might wean us from our consumer habits. We might regain perspective. Even marriages might be healed, if husbands would walk hand-in-hand with their wives and children through a sylvan cathedral strewn with wildflowers. Children might be weaned away from cyber-fantasy to develop a taste for the glory of creation. Most important, the Creator might break through the defenses we have thrown up to shield us from pondering the great questions: Who? What? Why? How? How long?

Wishful thinking? Perhaps. After all, Mary Helen and I hadn't done too well ourselves. But that year we were determined to take time to watch spring steal over the hillsides as we walked the trails. Timing would be crucial. When all the signs proclaimed, "It's wildflower time," we'd ignore the phone, allow e-mail to pile up, leave letters unanswered and bills unpaid. We'd ruthlessly cancel our commitments.

We'd search out that hushed valley where a meandering brook gurgled its way past wild ginger and jack-in-the-pulpits. We'd hunt for tiny stands of dutchman's breeches or squirrel corn. We'd kneel down to smell the violets. We'd rest on a log while we feasted our eyes on a hillside covered with waving trilliums. We'd search for their red cousins. We'd try to find starflowers, toothwort, bellflowers, and Solomon's seal.

But then, like every year before, the demands of society besieged our plans. We fought valiantly to break free—and we did manage to set aside several days to wander in the woodlands. We discovered a new flower and we tasted tranquility!

We would like to propose a new holiday—Wildflower Week. It would revolutionize western civilization!

> It is not growing like a tree
> In bulk, doth make man better be;
> Or standing long an oak, three hundred year,
> To fall a log at last, dry, bald, and sear:
> A lily of a day
> Is fairer far in May,
> Although it fall and die that night—
> It was the plant and flower of Light.
> In small proportions we just beauties see,
> And in short measures life may perfect be.[81]

Fudge's Mill

No more will the big wheel revolve with a clatter,
No more the bolts turn with a turbulent clank,
As down the dim flume rush the wonderful water
To burst forth in foam by the green covered bank.[82]

As a boy, "The Old Mill" on the Humber River in Toronto fascinated me—not the restaurant catering to upscale shindigs, but the decaying walls of the burnt-out building with the historical plaque. I could almost imagine the rush of water and the clank of pulleys. Since those dreamy days of childhood, five decades have trickled and surged, floated and raced by. Now, I find myself returning to that boyhood fascination. We live within twenty minutes of two water-driven sawmills and a functioning gristmill. The nearest is Fudge's Mill.

Intrigued by a road sign which read, "Grist Mill Road," we decided to explore. Cresting a rise, we coasted down a steep incline toward the east branch of the Ganaraska River. Before our eyes, a 19th century panorama unfolded. On the left, a white cottage surrounded by gardens stood on the banks of a tranquil pond fringed with willows. The pond's mirrored surface was fissured by foraging geese and ducks diving for tidbits. On the right, a weathered mill leaned west. We heard the rush of water down the millrace and the clank of old machinery as we rattled over the rickety wooden bridge past the mill.

Strange sights and sounds drew us to the mill: rusty tin roofing, the rattle of machinery, gaps in its tin sheathing, the slurp of imprisoned water, the battered pickup parked by the open doorway.

We wandered inside over boards scarred by the boots of a thousand farmers. We gazed around at strange pieces of machinery, at pulleys and shafts and old leather belts and levers and chutes, at timber framing draped with cobwebs, at sunlight glinting through gaps in the wall, at the floor tilting towards the millrace, sacks of feed, old boards, and bits of rusting iron in a corner.

Bob Fudge was filling a bag with feed from a chute. Another bag rested on the old weigh scale set into the floor. A bearded farmer chatted about goats and turkeys. The scene was so nostalgic that I peeked outside to see if Clarence and Mae were going by in their old pickup. This must be one of the places on their weekly tour of past haunts.

Bob was short and trim with corded arms used to manhandling heavy weights. He wore glasses and a perpetual grin. The whiskers on the grizzled dog of mysterious ancestry at his feet matched the grey strands that escaped from the baseball cap on his head. When we had a chance to chat, Bob told us about his dream of owning a gristmill before he even knew what a gristmill was. Seeing it, we were more tempted to call it a nightmare. Why would anyone leave a secure life in boomtown to throw his energies into saving such a ramshackle relic?

Mind you, sawmills and gristmills wrote much of the history of southern Ontario. Settlements sprang up where millers and sawyers could harness waterpower. Even on the relatively small Ganaraska watershed, historians estimate that there were anywhere from twenty-two to forty-seven mills. Our little village of Garden Hill boasted three, not including Fudge's Mill. Built in the 1850s, the original structure—a 35 x 30 foot timber-framed building—was washed away in a flood in 1902 and then rebuilt on the same foundations. In 1940, the building was expanded northward over the millrace. A water turbine replaced the water wheel and local farmers paid for the addition of a seed-cleaning machine. During the decades that followed, the mill continued to supply area farmers needing grain cleaned and cracked, and feed mixed to their specifications.

Fudge's Mill

In March of 1990, when Bob topped the rise leading down to the mill, he saw a sight that duplicated a vivid dream of a mill surrounded by dark water that he had had six months earlier.

Mr. Morrisy, the owner at that time, stood by the bridge, eyeing with anxiety the ice and high water. Pulling off the road, Bob got out and walked over. Mr. Morrisy asked, "Who are you?"

"I'm the man who is going to buy this. What is it?" Bob replied, thinking of a second dream in which he had seen himself running this very mill.

Startled, Morrisy responded, "Why, it's a grist mill!"

"What's a grist mill?" Fudge queried.

Immediately following this strange providence, he contacted his agent and commissioned him to make one offer and one offer only. Within twenty-four hours, a previous buyer had withdrawn his bid and Bob's had been accepted. From that day, June 15, 1990, he has not looked back. He believes God has led him here.

It's hard to argue with that conclusion. His dream of a mill, had been preceded by a trio of much more personal dreams following a car accident. These confronted him with his mortality, a vision of a yawning chasm of chaos, and the reality of God— a presence that radiated a love he had never experienced. Shaken, he determined to reform. Then he met Carol and they began seeing each other. As Bob got to know Carol and her friends, he recognized in them a lifestyle foreign to his own—a lifestyle founded upon a faith in God that he envied. He concluded that the dream was from God. He opened his personality to God's love in the person of Jesus.

With the help of Carol, and his new friends, he slowly began a journey. The journey was not without its twists and turns. Indeed, before long he and Carol had broken up.

It was during that period that he came upon the mill for the first time—and bought it. But he had a full time job and he didn't know the first thing about running a mill! Fortunately, before he turned over the mill, the previous owner spent six months training him on Saturdays. Now Bob knows every belt and pulley, every lever and chute. He talks as if he was a born miller.

"There are 13 feet of head at the intake. Running the turbine all day can reduce the pond by a foot. It's an amazing system. The mill was designed to take a wagonload at a time. It can never be overfilled. Yet I've stored up to 12 tons of grain on the second floor... If you want your chickens to be lean, you add no more than 5 percent corn to the mix—but to make them golden and fat, you add more corn. Farmers want extra corn, too, when they fatten up their cattle for market. By the way, chickens can't eat anything mouldy and turkeys..."

He described how the Crippen screening machine separates dirt and weed seeds from the various kinds of grain: wheat, barley, corn, oats, soybeans. Bob explained how to treat seed with Vitaflow 580 so rodents are repelled and germination is enhanced. He knows the function of each chute with its endless belt of cups, each shaft, each pulley, and lever. He learned all this, and kept the mill going, while maintaining a full-time job in Whitby, 40 miles away.

"Bob is there any money in it?" I queried.

"Well, not really. I'm a sub-dealer for an agro-company. But the big farmers go to the giant mills these days, where moisture and mixtures are computer-controlled down to a fraction of a percent. Besides that, many of them have their own hammer mills. I sell mostly to small farmers looking for feed for chickens, goats, and sheep. I also sell pet food and birdseed, binder twine, seed and salt for the cattle. Oh, there's not a lot of money in it and there is always something to do, something to repair—but it's fabulous here. I love it."

After he settled into a routine, romance blossomed again. He proposed to Carol and she accepted. Together, they fixed up the cottage and surrounded it with the lawns and gardens that slope down to the pond. It's beautiful and peaceful.

"Carol, have you ever regretted the move? Isn't it hard living like this?" I asked.

"No, we're happy here. The Lord has been good," she replied.

At a time when the steely eye of the developer too often stares down the misty eye of the heritage buff, it's heartening to know that there are folks like Bob and Carol Fudge around.

As we turned to leave, a kingfisher called from far down the pond. Inside the mill, a grey cat prowled the corners in its endless quest for mice. A strange white duck with a twisted red comb basked in the sun by the loading dock. A rusty truck pulled up for some feed. And the melody of water falling, water gurgling, water rushing down the millrace laid down a background sonata for this idyllic pastoral scene.

An honest miller hath a golden thumb.[83]

That Sensual Time of Year

Here is the land of quintessential passion,
Where in a wild throb Spring wells up with power.[84]

igh spring is the best of all times in the country—except
for summer, fall, early spring and the first snow. Well,
what can I say? I enjoy all the seasons. But late spring is a sensual time. Yes, thoughts turn to love. The hormones begin to
sing. But that's not exactly what I have in mind. Living in the
country seems to heighten all the senses, and we've got five.

Five full and fashioned senses, each
A fine precision instrument
To chart the wayward course
Through rock and moss
And riddles hard, or soft as ether, airy
Airy quite contrary
Where will the next wind blow?[85]

Leaving gasoline alley behind us, we drove north towards Turkey Hill. Soon both of us became aware of a subtle fragrance drifting in through the vents. It was lilac time again! Overnight, lilacs had burst into full bloom, flagging plots of land all over the province where pioneers had built their homesteads.

Scent. Throwing our windows open and slowing down to a crawl, we drank in the delicate fragrance. Lilac Lane, as we have come to call it, is a section of County Road 10 above Canton where enormous banks of lilac crowd the road. Usually, we speed through Canton, but during lilac time, we slow down to savour the scent. Spring seems to heighten our sense of smell.

True, fields spread with dung wrinkled our noses for a week or two. But as spring advanced the reek of manure quickly dissipated. Soon the sweet scent of clover wafted our way. Then waist high grasses heralded the season's first haying. And while the scent of freshly ploughed earth heralded early spring, the aroma of newly mown hay proclaimed high spring. Its pungent, country smell bespoke an abundance of fodder for the winter ahead. An early mowing meant another haying before summer faded. Giant checker pieces of coiled hay dotted the fields. Soon they would line fencerows, fill barns, and spill out into farmyards.

Touch. I've never been able to use those garden gloves they sell to protect your fingers from the dirt. Mind you, I need them in the fall when I split and stack wood. But that spring, I wanted to strangle the weeds with my fingers and feel the texture of the moist earth as I worked the flower beds and cultivated the vegetable garden. Unfortunately, through the spring and summer my finger nails began to look like those of a grease monkey.

Sound. No hum of traffic. No roar of transports. No wail of sirens. The odd rumble of a tractor. Robin and Robinette reproached us for evicting them from their nest on the garage door opener, a scolding tempered by their evening serenade. The chatter of our resident chipmunk. The bubbling of the bobolinks as they soared and dived. The raucous caw of crows in the pines below the house. The babble of goldfinch as they flocked around the feeder. Leaves rustled in the wind. Song sparrows laid down a symphony. Then silence. The crash of thunder as a spring storm swept across the land. The drumming of rain on the roof. The lively sounds of spring.

Taste. Tantalizing flavours to tempt the jaded winter palate. The savour of lightly steamed asparagus kissed by creamery butter—asparagus cut within the hour from a village garden. The sweet tang of the first radishes. Rich, green spinach picked and popped in the pot a few minutes before supper. Spring onions and a sprig of dill in a salad made from the tenderest, tastiest lettuce of the year.

Summer was peeking over the horizon when Mary Helen proclaimed, "Strawberries are ready!" Throwing some baskets in the car we headed over to the next concession. We turned in at a local farm, followed the signs to the strawberry patch, and joined other pickers getting their knees dirty and their lips red. Picking your own fresh strawberries without driving an hour through strangling traffic has to be one of country living's crowning delights.

Returning home in triumph, we immediately prepared a feast. But whether to mash them or slice them presented a dilemma. Mary Helen and I differ on the best way to savour strawberries. She maintains that to really enjoy spring strawberries, you must mash them up and heap them on short cake or biscuits. Then you add a dollop of whipped cream. Horrified at this attempt to drown their flavour, I insisted on cutting them up, sprinkling them with sugar, and pouring on a touch of milk. We are at least agreed on the mystic ability of homemade strawberry jam to add sunshine to a wintry day. So Mary Helen dedicated the rest of the day to jam making.

Sight. Ah, the sights of spring. Along every country concession a banner of wild grasses waved to passing travelers. A tint
of russet frosted the tops of this undulating roadside pennant.
Clumps of daisies and patches of clover nodded in the breeze.
Tiny yellow flowers crept onto the roadway. Banks of vetch tinted the fencerows with violet.

In mid-June we drove over to the village of Millbrook to
watch the parade celebrating the opening of their spring fair.
Finding a spot under the shadow of century-old buildings we
settled down to watch. A modern ladder truck and a big pumper
led the parade. They were followed by an antique fire truck lovingly waxed by volunteer firemen. A couple of prancing palomi-
nos tossed their manes. A collie pulled a miniature covered
wagon occupied by a little boy. Cheers erupted from spectators
as the local softball team strutted their stuff. Then an ancient
Plymouth chugged by followed by a fifties Caddie with enormous tail fins. There were old trucks, antique tractors, a convertible with a beauty queen waving to the crowd.

Parade in Millbrook

People in the throng shouted greetings and comments as
each entrant marched by. Everyone seemed to know everyone

else. A gaggle of girls and boys from the local daycare centre straggled along behind a big Raggedy Ann look-a-like. The mother of a wee girl dressed as Little Bo Peep tried vainly to control a very distracted lamb. The mayor glad-handed his way up the street. As the tail end of the parade passed them, spectators followed them to the fairgrounds.

On our return home, we headed out for our evening walk down Trespass Road. Duke bounded across the field to join us. "Isn't that sunset unbelievable?" I whispered quietly, awestruck by the impressionist canvas spread across the western sky.

"What's that colour? Salmon pink? And look at that long streak of soldier blue," Mary Helen responded.

Ever since her craft business, she has had very definite ideas about colours. My biases hark back to the names printed on the tubes of oil paint used by my mother. Our debate about shades and tints petered out as we fell silent under the spell of another country sunset. The blues deepened. Hints of violet appeared. Gold gilded the pink.

Duke searched for the scent of raccoons as we continued down Trespass Road through our private cathedral of arching maples and oaks. "Shsh," Mary Helen whispered, pointing ahead to a deer standing like a sentinel on the road ahead of us. With a bound it leapt the fence, its white tail signaling its flight through the grain. As if to mark the ending of another perfect late-spring day, a golden moon appeared through a curtain of cloud to the east. Ah, the sensual pleasures of high spring!

Sweet day, so cool, so calm, so bright,
The bridal of the earth and sky

Sweet spring, full of sweet days and roses,
A box where sweets compacted lie.[86]

SUMMER

The Value of an Occasional Indulgence

*To the body and mind which have been cramped
by noxious work or company,
nature is medicinal and restores their tone.
The tradesman, the attorney comes out of the din and craft
of the street,
and sees the sky and the woods, and is a man again.
In their eternal calm, he finds himself.
The health of the eye seems to demand a horizon.*[87]

The summer landscape was a lush patchwork of multiple shades of green. The lilacs had flowered and faded. Asparagus time had come and gone. A field of oats waved gently in the breeze and if you listened very closely, you could hear the corn growing. Signs advertising strawberry socials papered the window at the Garden Hill Store. But something was missing.

Where was the chip truck that sets up shop about this time every year? Had our young entrepreneur given up her dream of a college nest egg? Could her dad have sold it? A village summer without a chip truck? Grim thought indeed.

Of course, there still was Rosies' down by the Ganaraska in Port Hope where the fishermen gather. Another lured motorists at the crossroads near Gore's Landing with its aroma of fresh fries. I could have even detoured along Taunton Road to the blue bus or gone on to the chip truck near Orono. I could have faked a business trip to Cobourg to stop by the one offering free french fries with every thirteenth purchase.

The real sign that summer in southern Ontario has arrived—a country summer that is—is the appearance of chip trucks in the land. Now, I know some of you are aghast. You want to lecture me about all that cholesterol and other horrible stuff. But what is life without an occasional indulgence?

Unfortunately, at that time the TV news was running a series on health again. I sank deeper and deeper into the old recliner as I watched a reporter wax apocalyptic about the dangers of fat, of salt, of cholesterol, of saturates, of sugar, of... I couldn't keep track of it all. Too much this. Too little of that. Bewildering. And neatly slotted in between reports of murder and mayhem.

Don't get the wrong idea. I've always been years ahead of those health nuts. I've loved vegetables since I was a child. My eyes light up when you talk of corn or asparagus or carrots or cabbage or spinach or lettuce or radishes... you get the idea. I love vegetables but aren't potatoes a vegetable?

"Surely, once in a while we need to indulge ourselves," I thought as I slipped out of the house to go down to the village to get some gas. As I turned west a welcome sight appeared. The chip truck had returned! The tantalizing aroma of fries drifted in through the open window. I pulled up and nonchalantly sauntered over, making sure no neighbour was watching who could report my misdeeds to Mary Helen. "What'll it be sir?"

"Oh, just a small order of fries," I replied. Small, I want you to note, even though an elephant-sized order was only seventy-five cents more. What restraint!

I paced up and down impatiently as I waited. I wondered if Mary Helen had guessed my destination. I was already feeling a wee bit sheepish, but my overactive taste buds soon drowned out any guilt.

"Ready, sir," the teenage chef called.

U-m-m. No salt, I'm on a salt-free diet, after all. And a generous sprinkling of malt vinegar. None of that ketchup stuff. I didn't want to drown out the flavour of the season's first, fresh-cut french fries.

Author indulging himself

Carefully propping my treasure in the cup holder, I drove over to the pond where I could savour my indulgence. Two swans sailed by. Some geese honked in the distance. A kingfisher dove for fish. Ah, this is what summer in the country ought to be. The lazy warmth of the sun, a gentle breeze rippling the water, and the taste of crisp fries. That day a new project was born, research for a guidebook on the best chip trucks in southern Ontario.

Fortunately, my research on our love affair with *patate frites*, french fries, spuds, chips, and poutine was already underway. While interviewing entrepreneurs for a business newsletter, I had discovered Glynn Comeau, the *Spud King*.

Nine years previous, Glynn and Rhonda Comeau had a new home, a new baby—but no jobs. Today, Glynn owns a business that sells over a million dollars worth of pre-cut fries every year! What happened?

Everything looked rosy in 1991 when Glynn was twenty-five. Both had good jobs, Rhonda in accounting and Glynn managing a restaurant. With their first child on the way, they decided she would quit her job and they would buy their first home. On the Monday after the papers were signed, Glynn returned to work only to discover new owners who didn't need a manager. Overnight he was out of work with a mortgage payment coming due!

First he delivered pizzas, then he worked in a chip truck. While peeling and hand-cutting mounds of spuds, an idea began to germinate. Why not supply other chip trucks and restaurants with fresh-cut chips?

This idea became the embryo for *The Spud Factory*. At night, Glynn and his wife worked until 4:00 a.m. peeling mountains of potatoes and filling pails with fresh-cut chips. After four hours' sleep, Glynn would hop in a beat-up old Honda to serve customers in surrounding towns. It was touch and go. If his customers did not pay in cash, he was unable to buy the potatoes on the way home for the next day's orders. And his clientele, dissatisfied with oxidation of the chips, urged him to improve the product.

Using the chip truck—which he now owned—Glynn and Rhonda began to blanch the raw chips. Limitations in space and capacity forced them to buy restaurant fryers. Peeling, cutting, blanching, packing in pails—the whole process was very labour intensive. By hiring several helpers he was able to boost production to 300 pounds an hour of blanched fries.

As quality improved, demand for his product mushroomed. He has been able to develop a process that delivers chips of such quality and shelf life that chefs of major chains across Canada have been clamouring for his product. His chips taste just like home-made fries, even after being stored for three weeks.

A shift to an industrial mall in Cobourg, where they began using a commercial fryer, vastly increased their production. Glynn credits his accomplishments to a lot of lucky breaks and loyal employees, but I sensed that his success was more due to hard work and an ability to innovate.

Another small town story of success! Glynn Comeau combines vision, optimism, and the ability to inspire confidence in others, with innovative skills and hard work—key qualities of today's entrepreneurs of which we see a lot in the country.

Small towns and rural areas seem to inspire entrepreneurs as much as cities. The L.L. Bean empire is run out of Freeport, Maine. Walmart's headquarters is in Bentonville, Arkansas. The McCain frozen food conglomerate works from Florenceville, New Brunswick. Award-winning Horizon Plastics calls Cobourg home. The Nautical Electronic Laboratory which supplies about 30 percent of the global market in AM and FM radio transmitters operates out of Hackett's Cove, Nova Scotia.

The same countryside that prepared farm-bred people of rugged strength to fuel the industrial revolution has continued to spawn entrepreneurs. Rural living seems to inspire creative thought. No wonder many are returning to those open spaces where the sky springs free.

As Jack Lessinger brings out in his stimulating book, *Penturbia*, we are in the midst of a major migration of people from urban to rural areas.

A new vision of the good life... recycled from nostalgic old towns distant from major metropolitan areas, it thrives among pine-covered hills and peaceful neighbourhoods. A simpler, less materialistic life beckons. We drink in the sweet air, listen to the birdsong, and know that this is where our future hangs more golden than anywhere else.[88]

Among those who listen to the siren call to rural living are many of our most gifted innovators. Not infrequently, country living animates the kind of entrepreneurial vision that drives the new socio-economy. Far from being simply a fixation on nostalgia, the migration to small towns and rural destinations is viewed by many thoughtful people as a renewed commitment to the future.

As Glynn has shown, even in a field as mundane as spuds, there are business opportunities. And with my weakness for french fries, I'm glad the Spud King operates from a nearby town.

Garden Warfare

In goodly faith we plant the seed,
Tomorrow morn we reap the weed.[89]

E very year I'm faced with a mystery. It is not "the sweet mystery of life," but more like what theologians call, "the mystery of iniquity." Where do all the weeds come from? Why does every bug in the county zero in on my garden?

I love gardens. To even approach contentment, I have to have some flowers, some grass, some veggies—and of course, a few hundred trees. So every spring I till the soil, plant the seeds, and wait for Eden. Instead I get garden warfare.

It's not as if I don't try. I cultivate the vegetable patch deeply, work in some manure, lay out my rows of peppers, tomatoes, potatoes, corn, beans—you know, the whole cornucopia. Then I move to the flower beds. On hands and knees I get rid of the winter debris. I scuffle the soil carefully with a hand trowel, divide plants that have grown too large, move things around. I lovingly work in bone meal and discard every germinating weed.

But as soon as I turn my back the enemy infiltrates. When we went away for a week I returned to find a million weeds sprouting along with the carrots and radishes. Grass choked the scallions and threatened the tomatoes. In a frenzy, I attacked the enemy until the light failed, but the battle seemed hopeless.

I took heart though, when I heard the old Ford pickup rattling down Trespass Road toward me. Looking up, I caught Clarence and Mae peering at me as I gathered up my tools. As they rattled by at 15 mph, I detected them approvingly nod to each other. Somehow, I felt vindicated. As if I was part of a brotherhood stretching back to Eden: the eternal struggle against chaos. And as I surveyed the rows of weed-free carrots and tomatoes, I felt a sense of pride that I hadn't dishonoured my ancestors.

Returning limp and worn from the battle, I collapsed in my worn-out old chair. Mary Helen came over and pointed out, rather pragmatically, "Honey, you don't have time for so much garden. Why don't you get rid of that flower bed by the deck and the big one in front of the garage? You should cut back on the vegetables. You're getting too old for all this."

"Too old?" Mary Helen is so annoyingly rational, so practical. But to say I'm too old? Those were fighting words. She obviously didn't yet understand the male conquest gene. "I'm not going to let a few weeds and bugs beat me," I muttered to myself, as I squared off for the conflict ahead. What man can resist a challenge? I could almost hear the gardener's battle cry.

And so the summer progressed. At times I was almost tempted to purloin the title used by Robertson Davies' fictional character, Samuel Marchbanks, and change the name of our plot from Hemlock Meadow to *The Marchbanks Weed Sanctuary*.[90]

Admitting grudgingly Mary Helen's wisdom, I did cut back

by turning several flower beds close to the house into weed-resistant beds of decorative rock and broken terracotta.

Then the vegetables began to flourish. The spinach was scrumptious. "Honey, don't you love my spinach?" I couldn't help jabbing Mary Helen a little as she savoured one of her favourite vegetables. The beans came into flower. The tomatoes became luxurious. Corn stretched towards the sky. The raspberry patch looked promising. The potatoes... the potatoes were covered with beetles!

Where did they come from? There were no potato fields for miles. How could they suddenly appear overnight to munch away on my spuds? Who sent them an e-mail? Trying to avoid insecticides, I drowned them one by one in a soup can full of old motor oil. Unfortunately, as I soon discovered, the Colorado Potato Beetles brought with them a host of creeping, crawling, jumping, flying fiends.

A morning or so later I found, to my dismay, that several tomato plants had been stripped of their leaves. I searched for the culprit almost in vain until I discovered an enormous caterpillar dressed in combat camouflage having an early breakfast of one of my green tomatoes. With the enemy in my sights I extended my search and found half a dozen more. Squish. Squish. Every morning for days, I woke, fortified myself with a coffee, and ventured forth to check—only to discover more massacred tomato plants. Then suddenly the caterpillars disappeared leaving only their droppings as evidence of their depredations. I faced an entomological mystery. Where had they gone? I didn't tumble to the solution until I caught sight of foraging birds picking my plants clean. The whole experience gave me a heightened appreciation for ecological balance.

The birds couldn't do anything about underground grubs though. My last row of radish had been turned into subterranean row houses for hordes of tiny grubs. And they had begun to attack the carrots! Grasshoppers and slugs and crickets and aphids began to multiply. Fortunately, so did ladybugs and praying mantis, the bobcats and wolves of insect land. My increased appreciation for insect-eating birds made me more observant. I noticed that when I cut the grass a flock of swallows would often swoop and dive after the insects I disturbed. So I took care not to scare off the barn swallows that nest under the eaves of the garage.

I tried not to inhibit nature with chemical sprays and dusts.

Praying mantis

When I read that you can repel insects by planting marigold and garlic around the garden I took the bait. Soon I had a thriving row of garlic and bushy marigolds here and there. But I couldn't detect any appreciable decrease in the insect population! The marigolds seemed to just take up space. They didn't even flower very well. At least we could use the garlic.

It's a puzzle though. Why do the most beautiful flowers and the most delicious vegetables seem to have so many pests? Why don't they pick on the quack grass and the golden rod? I even had aphids attacking my lupins and crickets feasting on my beans. I had black spot on the roses and patches of dead grass where white grubs had been grazing below the surface of the lawn.

These grubs must taste like shrimp to the skunks. Every night skunks tore up patches of lawn and uprooted flowers for their shrimp cocktails. One evening when we returned home late, we cornered a culprit in the headlights. Not being foolish enough to challenge his (her?) hegemony over our lawn we shut off the engine and let our resident skunk saunter away. I just wish the smelly beasty wouldn't peek in the open window when I'm up late at night. Those knowledgeable in woodcraft assert that skunks are very well behaved and rarely spray people. But after trying to clean up my dog with cans and cans of tomato juice as a boy, I didn't want to put their restraint to the test.

During our first few years here, the raccoons turned up their noses at my spindly corn. Reasoning that I had been scratched off their itinerary I set to work fertilizing and pampering a new crop of corn. I took great pride in watching the ears swell and ripen. Then, just when I had decided to pick it the following day, coons arrived by moonlight to sample and scatter the best ears. How did they know that the corn was at its peak? Sweet, juicy, tender? Why hadn't they satisfied their passion by feasting on the huge field across the road? Another mystery.

It was too much—enough to make me abandon gardening and take up golf. But I couldn't forget those days when the computer screen stared at me blankly until I gained new inspiration from wandering through the garden. Daisies and black-eyed Susans waved gently in the breeze. The rose bush offered a perfect pink rose for my inspection. A monarch butterfly sipped nectar from the purple coneflowers. The perennial phlox were in their glory—giant red and orange and pink and white clusters. The miniature asters had begun to bloom. A bumper crop of grapes hung in clusters from the arbour.

Then there were the evening meals when we feasted on fresh beans and broccoli, the midnight sandwiches made of huge slices of vine-ripened tomatoes. You can talk about your lobster thermador but give me a fresh cob of corn, a mess of tender beans and tiny carrots, a plate of vine-ripened tomatoes and sliced cucumbers, steamed new potatoes smothered in creamery butter. Memories like those are enough to carry one through the winter only to awaken with fresh vigour every spring as the sun warms the soil.

I can't imagine myself living without some kind of garden. Even when we lived in a house with a walled and paved court-yard in a little town in Asia, I tore up some of the paving stones to plant flowers. After all, God is a gardener. And we live between two gardens; the Garden of Eden and the Garden by the crystal river in the everlasting. Between those two perfections, we may have garden warfare, but we also have periods of rapture.

Now the Lord God had planted a garden in the east, in Eden; and there he put the man he had formed. And the LORD God made all kinds of trees grow out of the ground—trees that were pleasing to eye and good for food... [he] put him in the Garden of Eden to work it and take care of it.[91]

On each side of the river stood the tree of life,
bearing twelve crops of fruit, yielding its fruit every month.
And the leaves of the tree are for the healing of the nations.
No longer will there be any curse.[92]

Bargain Breakfast

The rich and powerful of this land often establish
themselves in some plush five-star restaurant,
surrounded by their toadies.
[They] might have fared better in the polls
if they had held court
in one of the village restaurants of the nation,
where opinion is served up fresh and simple,
like the food.[93]

The sandwich board on the sidewalk caught our attention: "Breakfast Special - $2.99." The growling of our stomachs smothered any rational thought that this was just another heartburn café. Going inside, we noted that the two rows of tables with their checkered tablecloths looked clean. The vases of dried grasses and flowers bespoke a proprietor with more than the ordinary sense of style. The attractive décor raised our hopes again that we might have discovered a gastronomical gold mine.

Picking a table half way down, we glanced around. A black-board listed the day's specials: "Liver and onions, $5.95, Peameal bacon and eggs, $5.95, Hamburg steak, $6.95." No marks for originality.

At one table a retired couple scanned the newspaper as they finished off their coffee. At another, a lawyer-type with a fur-rowed brow munched toast while he made notes on a yellow legal pad. The stooped, gray-haired woman in an oversize coat at the very back cradled her coffee cup in her wrinkled fingers as if she was afraid it might be taken.

"I'll be right with you dearie," the waitress sang out cheeri-ly as she sailed by us with three plates balanced on one arm and a coffeepot in her free hand.

All of five-foot-five, she sported a gingham apron, culottes, and no-nonsense brogues. The laugh wrinkles on her round face accentuated her dancing brown eyes. A pencil peeked out of her tightly wound bun. Mid-fifties, I guessed. Not really pretty, and yet there was something attractive about her rather solid frame. We later learned that she was both a partner in the restaurant and waitress.

Returning to our table she commented, "Still raining out there? They say it will clear up later. How about some coffee?"

Nodding our heads for coffee, I rejoined, "We've had such marvelous weather. A day of rain won't hurt us."

When she returned with coffee, Mary Helen queried, "What's included in the breakfast special?"

"Three eggs. Bacon, sausage, or ham. Home fries. Toast."

"I'll have brown toast, eggs over medium, and bacon."

"And I'll have, let me see... white toast, scrambled eggs, and... make mine sausage," Mary Helen added.

As I savoured the day's first cup of coffee, I couldn't keep from peering around again. Miss Congeniality had stopped at another table on her way to the kitchen. "How did the week-end go?" she inquired. I missed the answer.

She seemed to know everyone except us—we hadn't been here before. A businessman with a grizzled beard and a dark suit went directly to the back counter to pick up his morning coffee. At a table on the far side a woman dressed in a navy suit leafed through a pile of folders. Real estate agent, I concluded, as I watched her light up a filter tip and begin to scribble notes on a pad.

Two women came in and sat down at the next table. They proceeded to systematically lay out an assortment of lottery cards: three or four Nevadas, a card I couldn't recognize and a Bingo card with an elaborate assortment of boxes hidden by that mysterious grey gloop that keeps secret numbers secret. Without asking, Ms. Sunshine brought them a coffee and chatted about the latest lotto jackpot.

"I was one number off!" the older woman with the short dark hair and the jogging suit replied. "Just bring me toast this morning, Hild."

"I'll have the usual," said the other woman with the perfectly styled hair as she extracted a lighter and cigarettes from her expensive purse.

"Stop staring," Mary Helen whispered. "You haven't heard a word I've said!"

With a guilty start, I realized her comments about our plans for the rest of the day had gone completely over my head.

Fortunately, at that moment, "Hild" brought our plates. Umm... crisp fresh-cut home fries; eggs done perfectly, not swimming in grease; bacon, crisp and succulent, not limp and fatty like at the last place we ate; lightly buttered brown toast with three choices of jam!

I attacked my plate with gusto while I carried on a desultory conversation with Mary Helen. "This is really good. The home fries are crisp, the bacon is wonderful. How are you doing?"

"The coffee's a bit weak, but everything else is great. How would you rate this place?" she replied.

"I'd give it an eight. Even paying extra for the coffee, the price is amazing. The smoking is a bit of a problem."

We rate the places where we eat on a scale of one to ten. This one would call for return visits. No wonder almost every table was filled.

Engrossed in savouring my last strip of bacon and slathering jam on my last wedge of toast, I had lost track of the women at the next table. When I finished off, I glanced over. Their now useless Nevada cards lay in two orderly piles on the table. They had opened all the little cardboard windows without uttering any yelp of pleasure. At that point they were busily engaged in using a spoon to scrape the grey goop off their Bingo cards. Their concentration telegraphed intense thought and care. Finally, one of them sighed, "Only two."

I had no idea what she meant, but it didn't sound very encouraging. Both had little leather pouches in which to keep their lottery brick-a-brack. I got the impression that they joined forces every Monday to brave the tempestuous Sea of Fortune in search of Jackpot Island.

"I can't eat all these home fries," interjected Mary Helen as she scooped some onto my plate.

While I was cleaning them up, the waitress disappeared out the front door. "What can she be doing?" I wondered. "Did she forget to buy enough bacon? Is she going to get the daily paper?" A few minutes later she returned with several lottery tickets clutched in her hand. Smiling at us as she sailed by, she said, "I'll be right back with more coffee, darling."

As we sipped our java, we chatted quietly about the gambling fever we meet wherever we go. Nothing like a good breakfast to promote deep thought! We wondered why such a likeable and hard-working woman, committed to offering high quality, if simple, meals for a reasonable price would buy lottery tickets. Why not continue to build on her loyal clientele rather than venture forth, hand-in-hand with Lady Luck? Was she dreaming of a jackpot that would buy her a condo in the Caribbean?

We could understand the appeal. Every week the media highlight some new millionaire, like the twenty-two-year-old student who won millions and retired before she even graduated. Who can resist the appeal of our governments, our hospitals, our civic clubs, and even our sports teams who all push us to do our civic duty by buying a ticket to a golden future while investing in "community improvement"?

We can't seem to escape gambling fever: line-ups in the mall, appeals from civic clubs to buy tickets on a new Bronco or a trip to Hawaii, ads on TV and radio, neighbours indulging their hopes at Gary's store, mail campaigns, even a sales pitch from the proprietor of the convenience store in town when I went in to buy a pop!

It's strange. North Americans have never had such a high standard of living. And yet, we've never had so little contentment. Living out here in the country, we are certainly not immune to this virus. We'd love a new car, new carpets, a more powerful computer, a TV with a bigger screen, a vacation in Bora Bora... have to stop that line of thought immediately! The itch is well nigh irresistible. Contentment seems almost subversive, as if fueling the capitalist economy by a continual drive to keep up with, or surpass, the Jones is our civic duty. And the most patriotic way to accelerate the process is to gamble.

Casinos. Lotteries. Break-open tickets. Bingo. Video lottery terminals. Slot machines. The political leaders who spent us into a swampland of infinite debt seem bent on luring us on into the quicksand of addictive gambling.

It's puzzling. We have such opportunities to achieve success through harnessing innovative technology and yet we choose to daydream. It's as if the whole world has returned to a mediaeval faith in wizards, genies, and witch doctors where fantasy hijacks pedestrian vocations and practical virtues.

It is passing strange that those who, on the one hand lampoon faith in God as primitive credulity, champion fantasies and fairy tales. We live at a time when our attempts to divorce ourselves from our Christian past are almost complete. Few today recognize the connection between faith in the Creator and the respect for creation and creature that spawned science and democracy. This loss of historic memory has harvested a whirlwind of diminished respect for many of the virtues it begat—including a solid work ethic.

Upon return home, we startled a chipmunk, cheeks full of seeds, as it scurried to line its larder for the coming winter. I wondered if the 21st century society's flirtation with gambling would require us some day to relearn the lessons about frugality and foresight that are so daily demonstrated by creatures as varied as ants and chipmunks.

Through our country window we have a ringside seat to view nature's dynamic drama. This gives us a better chance than many to reject fantasy and relearn from God's creatures virtues smothered by urbanization. Understand, I am not claiming that their asphyxiation was deliberate, or that the march of civilization did not encourage creativity, innovation, and allied virtues. "Progress" has greatly enriched our lives. Admittedly, it has helped many like us to cast off the urban girdle of concrete and steel. Nevertheless, out here we have an unusual opportunity to rediscover the joys to be found in the simple things of life, joys trampled by the march of progress. Consummate consumers that we are, this is no thanks to us.

> *Four things on earth are small, yet they are extremely wise:*
> *Ants are creatures of little strength,*
> *yet they store up their food in the summer;*
> *Coneys [rock badgers] are creatures of little power,*
> *yet they make their home in the crags;*
> *Locusts have no king, yet they advance together in rank;*
> *A lizard can be caught with the hand,*
> *yet it is found in king's palaces.*[94]

Purple coneflowers

Thunder on the Ridges

The wind changed every way and fled
Across the meadows and the wheat;
It whirled the swallow overhead,
And swung the daisies at my feet...

Took the maples by surprise,
And made the poplars clash and shiver,
And flung my hair about my eyes,
And sprang and blackened on the river.[95]

The crash of thunder woke me from a deep sleep. Flashes of lightning lit up the darkness. Rain pounded on the roof. I turned over and tried to go back to sleep. No use. Thunderous echoes and dazzling flashes filled the room. Slipping out of bed I checked the windows on the upper floor. Then I unplugged the computer in my office and the microwave in the kitchen before slipping into the living room to watch the spectacle through the picture window.

Streaks of lightning lit up the countryside. I could clearly see the forest half a mile away. Thunder rumbled and crashed and reverberated through the hills. The torrents of rain beating on the roof sounded like the cadences of a drummer beating out a tattoo. The rhythm of the rain rose and fell with the gusts of wind that drove it, sometimes flinging itself almost horizontally across the awakened land. I seemed to be immersed in some primeval concert from the dawn of creation, something like that which moved Haydn to write:

How now rage with fury, clouds and tempest.
Like chaff in the whirlwind fly storm-driven clouds.
The sky is cleft by fiery lightning,
Tremendous, awful, the thunder roll.
The floods give forth at His command
The rains and showers, all refreshing.[96]

Mary Helen joined me as I moved to the front door. Slipping outside, we stood engulfed in the storm, though sheltered under the wide overhang of the roof. Splashes of wind-driven rain wet our upturned faces and washed our extended hands. Rain pelted the flowers and pounded on the road. A flood poured through the downspouts and cascaded off the roof as the volume of water overwhelmed the eaves troughs. The driveway became a river and every flower bed a pond.

We had been enduring a hot, dry summer. The lawn was sere. The roadways were fringed in funereal brown. Corn in the field across the road looked stunted. The dirt in the flower-beds had turned to a powder that repelled my feeble attempts at watering. Concern was expressed about fire igniting the pine forests stretching west from our house. The Ganaraska River had shrunk into a wizened snake slithering through the bottomlands. Tonight, it would sing its rebirth as it became fat and full. And the thirsty land would turn green again.

"Isn't this glorious?" Mary Helen exclaimed. We felt like dancing a jig.

There is a rapture in tempestuous weather,
A sympathy with suffering, which thrills
When midnight mists around the mountains gather,
And hoarse winds howl among the moaning hills.[97]

We love storms. Not for us the choreographed terror of the roller coaster or even a great display of fireworks. Oh, we appreciate human expertise, but there is nothing like watching towering cumulo-nimbus clouds gallop across the sky.

As we watched the rain create a pond on our front lawn, we reflected on the marvel that is the Creator's water cycle. Our puny attempts all summer to water the flowers seemed laughable compared to the deluge falling in a few minutes from these clouds, clouds that towered ten miles into the air. Someone driven by statistics more than poetry has calculated that where rain falls at a rate of twenty-four inches per year, everyone receives 407,510 gallons of free water per acre!

It is astonishing to realize that all this water is collected and transported around the earth without benefit of pumps to move it or fires to evaporate it or refrigeration to condense it. Some years ago a Canadian physicist at the University of Alberta wrote:

A rain of four inches over an area of approximately 10,000 square miles would require the burning of 640,000,000 tons of coal to evaporate enough water for such a rain. To cool again the vapours thus produced and cause it to condense into clouds would require another 800,000,000 horsepower of refrigeration working day and night for one hundred days in order to produce rainfall equivalent to that mentioned.[98]

This calculation only applies to 10,000 square miles. Ontario has 412,579 square miles, forty-one times that amount of land and an average annual rainfall of between twenty-five and thirty-six inches. We find it hard to be blasé about summer storms.

Trying to imagine the amount of electrical energy loosed by the lightning flashes that we saw illuminating the night, increased our awe. A man in Massachusetts estimated that the electrical power required for one unusual display he witnessed was equivalent to one hundred million kilowatts, the equivalent of all the power generated in the U.S. at that time.[99]

Another writer has estimated that:

There are 1800 storms in operation at one time with about 100 flashes per second. The energy expended in these storms amounts to the almost inconceivable figure of 1,300,000,000 horsepower.[100]

We have revelled in the power of monsoon storms in the Himalayas and watched dust storms in the Sindh darken the sky at noonday. But we don't take them for granted. Several years ago on a warm summer day, I went into town on an errand. As usual, I left my computer on. While I was away a sudden storm enveloped the hills. Mary Helen had no warning of the approaching thunderstorm until the house suddenly shook under the power of a lightning strike perilously close to the house. Our neighbour happened to witness the enormous thunderbolt strike the earth. Instantly, power was lost and my computer fried. The surge also destroyed our microwave.

Fortunately, most of my files were backed up and insurance paid for a new computer and microwave. Nevertheless, some things were lost for good. And it took me several weeks to catch up.

Now, when I hear the crash of thunder, I urgently save my work and shut down the computer. In spite of a guaranteed surge system, I pull the plug. The possibility of losing a week's work has made me skittish.

In spite of the danger, we still love thunderstorms. Since someone has estimated that we are "bombarded by 16 million thunderstorms and two billion gallons of rain each year,"[101] we may as well learn to appreciate them. And so when one rolls over the hills as it did that night, we take a ringside seat and settle down to watch one of God's great spectacles.

How great is God—beyond our understanding!
The number of his years is past finding out.
He draws up the drops of water,
which distill as rain to the streams;
the clouds pour down their moisture
and abundant showers fall on mankind.

Who can understand how he spreads out the clouds,
how he thunders from his pavilion?
See how he scatters his lightning about him,
bathing the depths of the sea.

Listen! Listen to the roar of his voice,
to the rumbling that comes from his mouth.
He unleashes his lightning beneath the whole heaven
and sends it to the ends of the earth.
After that comes the sound of his roar;
He thunders with his majestic voice.[102]

4th Line Theatre production of "The Devil and Mr. Scriven"

Barnyard Theatre

To our mother's memory
We gather together to sing
She who planted the trees in rows to be
Like lines in a poem about spring

As we come to praise the first parents
Who lay down beneath the covering sky
And rose up with the key just so that we
Could make this garden our home till we die[103]

We sat expectantly on moveable bleachers facing a typical Ontario farmhouse from the last century: white clapboard, green trim, gingerbread, a tangle of old-fashioned shrubs ambled across the front and down the west side. Giant maples spread their canopy over the lawn where we sat. *The Orchard*, a play put on by the 4th Line Theatre, was about to begin. But there were no microphones, no painted backdrops, no stage but the front lawn of the house, the surrounding fields, the barnyard behind and the clouds above.

The spectators fell silent as a figure playing both a guitar and a mouth organ appeared to the right of the house. Throughout the play, he provided quiet background music. Valerie, a young woman dressed in work togs, strode in from the fields. She began to water a few petunias growing by the front steps. Then she methodically took off her barnyard shoes and carefully laced up a pair of '50s saddle shoes.

As she went about her duties, Valerie carried on a soliloquy describing the crisis facing the farm. She rehearsed her own sad story as an orphan adopted into the Andrews' family. Then she disappeared inside only to appear shortly on the second story balcony with its white pickets. There she proceeded to water some more straggly petunias. Tasks complete, she settled down to read a romance while she awaited the arrival of Lillian Andrews, the owner of the farm. Lillian had been away in California for years leaving the care of the rundown farm in Valerie's hands.

Suddenly a red convertible from the '60s roared up the drive to our right, circled the house and came to a screeching stop in front of the house. A plump, polyester-clad real estate agent unfolded himself from the car. Waving a bouquet of fading roses, Jack looked around for Lillian, his erstwhile flame. Spotting Valerie on the balcony, he proceeded to pitch the wisdom of selling the farm to his developer chums before the bank could foreclose.

With guests from the US, we were attending the 4th Line Theatre's production of a locally written play called, The Orchard. Like many, we often put off visits to local events until out-of-town visitors arrive. We had wanted to attend this theatre for years, but something always came up.

Productions on the 4th Line usually take place in the barnyard. Three barns, built by George Winslow 150 years ago, provide set, stage, and seating for this unique theatre. Canny settler that he was, he knew that by building the barns in a U shape facing south, the sun would be trapped and animals would be sheltered from the north winds. His foresight now shades spectators during July and August when most of the plays take place.

The idea for a rural "theatre in the round" germinated in the fertile imagination of George Winslow's great-great-grandson, Robert Winslow. Robert grew up on the family farm but his love of theatre took him to Edmonton where his career blossomed. Then the serious illness of his widowed mother brought him back to Ontario. When she died he pondered the fate of the farm. At the time, he was working on The Cavan Blazers, a play depicting an ugly chapter in local history. Protestant settlers had tried to drive Irish Catholics out of the township. Originally, he had planned to stage it in a conventional indoor theatre in the city. But with the innovative bent that is his hallmark, the idea suddenly came to him of presenting the play in his own barnyard. That was 1992. Clearing the barns of decades of manure, installing bleachers on one side, and staging the play took massive amounts of help from eager local volunteers and friends in the arts community. The theatre that began on a shoestring now attracts people from far and wide.

As I've already noted, the action doesn't only take place in the barnyard. Besides the farmhouse, the hills, vales, and woodlands often resound to sounds of thespians. One year Robert Winslow staged a battle from the 1837 Mackenzie Rebellion. The audience was ferried by a horse-drawn wagon to a log cabin in a woodland clearing. Moonlight has been used as a backdrop. Horseback riders have appeared over the crest of a hill galloping towards the audience. Vintage automobiles routinely rumble through the set, as do horses and the occasional live chicken.

The 4th Line Theatre's goal is:

> ...to preserve and promote our Canadian cultural heritage
> through the development and presentation of regionally based,
> environmentally staged historical dramas.[104]

"Fourth Line" is vintage Ontariospeak. Pioneer surveyors laid
out our townships in *lines* running east and west and *concessions*
running north and south. The Winslow farm sits on the 4th Line
of Cavan Township, 30 kilometres southwest of Peterborough.

The plays entertain. They also bring alive local history and
celebrate regional heroes. *The Great Farini* dramatized Billy
Hunt, the farm boy who ran away with the circus. In the late
1800s Hunt became an international celebrity by inventing the
human cannonball and doing stunts like crossing Niagara Falls
on a tightrope. *The Devil and Joseph Scriven* celebrated the local
teacher and evangelist who wrote one of the world's favourite
hymns, *What a Friend We Have in Jesus*.

The 4th Line Theatre dramatizes universal themes such as
the anguish of bigotry and the pain of lost love. Plays also highlight rural themes—the worries of farmers beset by weather and
bankers and the effects of technology on rural life. *The Orchard*,
the play we enjoyed with our guests, told the poignant tale of a:

> ...farm in decay, the bank about to foreclose, and hungry land
> developers hovering like vultures. Loosely based on Anton
> Chekhov's classic play, The Cherry Orchard, this moving drama
> transports the audience on a journey into the recent past, asking
> questions about ownership, freedom and a sense of place.[105]

While the actors may not have had the glitzy polish of Hollywood or Broadway, we sat entranced by the authenticity of the
scenes they conjured up under the great maples. With wild honking of horn, Lillian arrived in a vintage sedan. Conservative Valerie

and polyester Jake watched in amazement as the car disgorged its cargo. Lillian wore an ankle-length hippie dress with beads and kerchief. She danced across the grass in the arms of a bearded man who announced their intention of setting up a commune. At that point her estranged husband arrived in an old truck.

Through four scenes of hippie hilarity the pathos deepened. Sinister developers from big city Toronto turned up the pressure through their lovelorn lackey. But neither Lillian's naiveté nor her consort's rhetoric could forestall the rumble of the real-life bulldozer that ended the play.

As we drove away the beauty of the countryside washed over me. But I was somewhat sad. I wondered how long the villagers and farmers of Cavan Township could resist the pressure to develop and divide and pave. The play, and its setting, evoked a poignant sense of the incredible privilege of living so close to nature.

Sharon Butala asks similar questions in *The Perfection of the Morning*. She recounts her metamorphosis from a city-dwelling intellectual into a rancher's wife. It took some years for her to identify the shock she experienced upon moving to a new home in southwestern Saskatchewan. Under the tutelage of the living sky and the short grass prairie she experienced an epiphany. But, as drought decimated the land and grain prices plummeted, she and her husband Peter began to face the danger of expulsion from the land.

She knew that she could take up her city life again—but not without profound loss.

The plight of the farmers is directly related to the question of our need as a species to come back to Nature... reclaiming our lost souls... At the simplest level is the fact that all the values we cherish and that we consider to be the basis of our culture as a whole, and that provide for its continuity but that are difficult to keep alive in cities, live on in the country: tightly knit extended families and small communities, where the loss of any one member leaves a gap but where deviance is tolerated and doesn't mean a life on the streets, where interdependence is clear and co-operation thus a way of life, but without destroying self-reliance... [106]

She continues:

Each individual farmer knows his acres of land intimately, knows the weather patterns over it, knows what grows best where and why.... No society can afford to wipe out the whole class of people in whom the practical knowledge laboriously passed down by generations remains alive. [107]

Translated urbanites such as ourselves echo these sentiments. We earnestly hope that rural municipalities will increasingly treasure the natural wealth found within their boundaries. When they recognize their peculiar stewardship they will resist the temptation to dilute the zoning regulations designed to conserve farms and limit careless development.

As Butala faced the possibility of expulsion from the land, she wrote, "The greatest loss it seemed to me, was the loss of constant contact with Nature and all that implied." [108]

As the years unroll behind us, Mary Helen and I know that there will come a day when we will be compelled to sell Hemlock Meadow. All the more reason to cherish each day, to listen closely to birdsong and wind, to revel in the night sky, and to respect our farm neighbours.

The Dog Days of Summer

The harvest sun lay hot and strong
On waving grain and grain in sheaf,
On dusty highway stretched along,
On hill and vale, on stalk and leaf.[109]

The ground shuddered under the weight of a monster machine. I stood frozen in its path, unable to move. Jerking awake from a nightmare, I threw off the covers. The ground was vibrating. A deep rumble rattled the windows. Stumbling down the stairs and throwing open the front door, I caught sight of Big Bertha, Lev's combine growling by in the field of wheat across the road. Bertha stopped with a clank beside a pickup and a grain truck parked on the shoulder.

A cloudless sky stretched to the far horizon. The big red machine, shutting down with a cough and whimper, ejected a coverall-clad figure I recognized as Lev: heavy scarred boots, signature cap advertising co-op feeds, the stubble on his chin told its own story—too much to do and too little time between rainstorms.

Gesturing towards Big Bertha, he beckoned Marty, one of two neighbouring farmers who had evidently joined him for the harvest. With help scarce, two or three farmers share machines and expertise at times like these. Marty jumped up on the machine with him to adjust Bertha's cantankerous innards. After grunts, shouts for another wrench and much gesturing, Lev signalled Al, the other farmer, to start the beast. With a whine and whistle, Bertha rumbled to life again. Satisfied, Marty and Al jumped down and Lev began again his circuit of the fields.

The teeth of Bertha's voracious grain head cut great swathes through the wheat. Turning, grabbing, scissoring, thrashing— Bertha circled the field under his expert hands. When its hopper filled, he drove over to the grain truck, swung the auger into position, and directed a golden stream of wheat into the truck bed. While Lev returned to the harvest, Marty drove the grain truck to the grain elevator 15 miles away. Meanwhile Al jockeyed a string of grain carts into position with his tractor. After a morning interrupted by several breakdowns and long waits at the grain elevator, the field was reduced to stubble and Lev had money in the bank—hopefully, enough to stave off another year of red ink.

With Lev's wheat cut, the trio headed off to Al's farm where they would work well into the night. Up and down the concessions giant combines rumbled from field to field. Dozens of trucks lined the shoulder waiting their turn to unload at the elevator in Cavan. With the weatherman predicting hail and severe rainstorms for the next day, farmers throughout the county worked through the night. From our hill, we could see their headlights, like giant fireflies, twinkling in the darkness all over the valley.

The dog days of summer were upon us. Those hot days of harvest when farmers keep an eye on the sky and an ear to the weather reports. But for those of us fortunate enough to make our living in other ways, these are the lazy, hazy, wonderful days of summer when country living is blissful.

June was behind us. The daisies and tall blue gentians that waved in the breeze along the roadways were fading. The yellow and purple flowers of the vetch that fringed the fencerows had gone to seed. A new batch of strawberry jam was stored in the back of the cupboard. Fresh peas were a memory, their vines yellowing in the relentless sun.

Queen Anne's lace fringed the country roads eliciting rhapsodies from Mary Helen, as she exulted in one of her favourite wildflowers. I hadn't noticed them much, brought up as I was to view them as weeds. Here and there, patches of blue chicory and black-eyed Susans provided a colourful contrast.

The village pond lured families to picnic on its shore and paddle in its warm water. Fresh veggies attracted a steady stream of customers to the local vegetable stand. Dorothy's House Museum, a tiny little house with a marvelous collection of dolls and a drive shed sheltering an antique threshing machine, was open for summer visitors. But it couldn't compete with the ball-park across the road. Every night, the arc lights attracted softball aficionados from miles around. Country dwellers are almost as serious about softball as hockey.

Serious farmers, serious ball players, serious trenchermen are sometimes a little wild. Take Coulter's horses. Coulter's horses like to frolic with wild abandon. They frequently meander down one of the area concession roads. One morning in early summer Sam left home to head off to his early morning shift. When he rounded a corner he ran smack into Coulter's herd.

The OPP (Ontario Provincial Police) officer shook his head as he described the scene to Gary at the store. "Sam killed one of the horses outright. Another was injured so badly, we had to shoot it. But you should see Sam's car. It looks like he ran into a cement truck. Totaled. A write-off. Lucky for Sam, his airbag caught him. When we arrived he was limping around in a daze. He's bruised all over."

Country driving requires instant reflexes. You never know when you might round a curve on a winding road and come face to face with a clutch of frolicking fillies or Bossy looking for greener pastures or maybe even a herd of deer. But hey, this is country living and these things are expected during the dog days of summer.

How boring country life must seem to many: miles from a mall, no corner store, one gas station within a radius of 10 miles, 15 miles to get a refill on propane, no movie theatre for 30 miles—and the selection! And worst of all, no donut shops! How can we expect the police to do their duty in a donut-free township?

A few weeks after the case of the frolicking fillies, two OPP officers showed up at Gary's store when I arrived for butter and eggs. Out of the corner of my eye I watched them vary their donut diet with a selection of candy bars, chips, and pop.

Curious about the unusual build-up of police, I delayed my departure so I could pump Gary for the scoop when the officers left. "Two men walked into the school this morning when the caretaker was cleaning one of the portable classrooms. He thought they were school officials until later when he saw them peering in the window at the neighbouring farm. Immediately, he called 911. The farm wife had already hit the panic button."

Another customer chimed in. "They've already got 5 cruisers up there. And they just brought in a tracking dog and a couple of ATV's."

"They caught one of the guys right off the bat," Gary continued, "He's sitting in a cruiser but refusing to talk."

"Yeah. That cute blonde officer told me they are escapees from Alberta with a Canada-wide warrant on their heads."

As the day progressed a score of cruisers converged on our tiny village from counties all over Ontario to search for the remaining fugitive. This was no easy task since, just beyond the village, the Ganaraska Forest stretches west for 10 miles without a through road. When we saw a search helicopter criss-crossing the forest, we decided to postpone our walk that day. A couple of days later the fugitive was caught halfway across Ontario.

Excitement? You never know. And as August emptied into September we wondered where the next outrage would come from. Would one of our local characters parade down the middle of the Ganaraska Road in the buff while he tried to balance an empty whiskey bottle on his head? Would protests about the dirt bike races result in more mailboxes being trashed? Would plans to expand the pig farm on the hill create a township-wide stink? Would the councillors get a tongue-lashing for trying to sit on the fence? Would the new pay-per-bag garbage solution create a garbage rebellion?

The crisp evenings of early September signaled the advance of fall. Clumps of purple and violet and white appeared where wild asters blossomed among the goldenrod. Feathery grasses waved in the breeze. The bulrushes in the defile had become plump and brown. Fields of soybeans lay bronzed and ready for harvest. The ears of corn that had been pointing skyward were now drooping earthward. With the brilliant greens of spring a distant memory, the hills stood clothed in the faded and dusty garments of late summer. The whole countryside looked tired, washed out, as if it could hardly wait for the golden days of autumn.

> *The sky was a blue meadow in which clouds like lambs grazed slowly.*
> *This was what we had dreamed after.*
> *This was what we had worked for,*
> *the peace and quiet of a lonely concession line,*
> *the nearness of things eternal, and the time to savour them.*[110]

Market Mania

Have you tried zucchini:
in a stew, as a bread,
fried in butter,
stuffed with shrimp?
in a soup, as a salad, in a pickle?[111]

(Sign at the Guelph Farmer's Market)

The weekly shopping expedition is serious business—time stolen from productive activities to buy the necessities. People with sober expressions push shopping carts down the aisles of giant supermarkets while they cross items off their list. Agonizing decisions face them at every turn. Buy the sugar coated corn puffies or the fibre-enriched flakes, taste or health? Choosing from a hundred kinds of bread, a thousand kinds of soap, a million kinds of dog food. By the time you stagger out the door a hundred bucks poorer, your decider is worn out.

At the farmer's market shopping is fun. The choices are simple: peaches or plums, red potatoes or white, bowling ball cabbages or giant heads of cauliflower, three kinds of corn, homemade bread or fresh pies. People laugh, chat, look, sniff, pinch, eat—and most buy. Everyone is there, from octogenarians leaning on their canes to babies in strollers.

The first sight that greeted us at the Peterborough Farm Market was a mouth-watering display of peaches, grapes, and plums from the Niagara Peninsula. Too expensive, I cautioned, determined to compare prices before buying peaches for jam. Next came an enormous stall offering a bewildering selection of melons, peppers, onions, cucumbers and tomatoes—with samples to taste. The flies had been there first, so we declined.

Across the way a matron in a long dark skirt sold fudge. Beside her an old-timer showed a boy how to operate his handmade wooden windmills. Next came a young couple in their early twenties offering an array of vegetables. Heaps of cauliflower and broccoli. Carrots and peppers. Cucumbers and squash. Corn and potatoes. Across the way, a hillbilly look-alike strummed a banjo. His companion, a teen with a pony-tail and a ring through his lower lip, made his fiddle dance. The open banjo case held the odd coin or two.

A sign reading, "Music Garlic," stopped us in our tracks. "What is music garlic?" I asked the lady tidying her stall.

Not really answering my question, she replied, "My brother developed it. It has won prizes all over Canada. It's the best in the country." She pointed to an elderly couple at the other end of the stall selling a selection of vegetables from their home garden, probably to bolster a meager pension. "I come every Saturday to help them with their stall."

"But what makes this kind of garlic so good? Is it more aromatic, more pungent, bigger? What?"

"It's just the best."

Several stalls farther on, a burly man and his ten-year-old son sold mushrooms. There were white button mushrooms plus ten or twelve other varieties. "Where do you get so many mushrooms?" I queried.

"We grow them!" he expostulated, a trifle miffed to think that we might doubt their pedigree.

"Around here?" I said displaying my ignorance. "I thought they grew much farther south."

"Oh, no. We live up near Lakefield."

I was surprised to learn that north of Peterborough, on the very edge of Ontario's summer playground of lakes and cottages, a farmer was growing mushrooms. Obviously he made a good living in the process.

Farm market—selling corn from the trunk of a car

Some of the stalls were jerry-built affairs, the work of amateur gardeners and crafters. One man, whose roots clearly went back to the Great Depression, sold corn from the trunk of his old gas-guzzler. Other stalls showed the marks of professional design and construction.

The stall for Betty's Pies and Tarts was a specially-built van. We were surprised to see a Hallelujah Hill neighbour selling so far from home. Of course, we shouldn't have been. After all, people drive miles out of their way to buy the sausage-rolls and tarts, the bread and muffins she sells from her renovated garage on a hill in the middle of nowhere.

Mary Helen beckoned me over to a flower stall. "How do you keep the sunflowers from wilting? The ones I cut only last a day or two," she asked the lady sitting in the midst of a huge array of glads and sunflowers.

"The professionals freeze-dry them and send them all over the world," she replied. "But I dip the stems in boiling water as soon as I cut them. That makes them last. You can even dip the stems and then freeze them. When you bring them out of the freezer let them slowly come up to room temperature. They'll last for months."

Mary Helen bought a bunch to try, but missed some step in the freezing process for they only lasted a couple of days.

"Free kitten mister? And a free tin of cat food if you give it a home."

I turned to see an adorable kitten climbing up the shirt of a tousle-headed boy. His slightly older sister held out a tin of cat food. The boy's eyes were big and brown and pleading. "Here hold it," he pleaded.

Looking in Mary Helen's direction I replied, "Well, we do have mice." But the tilt of her head warned me it was a bad idea.

Assessing quickly the callused state of our hearts he turned to a girl coming toward him hand-in-hand with her grandfather. "Yuh wanna hold a kitten? Look how cute he is." They stopped and the girl reached out to pet the tiny tabby.

Mary Helen pulled me away before my resistance melted,

"Look honey," she exclaimed.

I followed, patting my wallet to make sure it was still there, knowing I was going to have to shell out. I expected to see a stall selling hand-sewn children's dresses or handcrafts of one kind or another. But instead I saw (I couldn't believe it... in Peterborough of all places!) a cart advertising curries, samosas, and other Asian delights. Four sari-clad women and a young girl in jeans ran the stall. A blackboard listed the kinds of curry they offered. One of the women was marking off curries no longer available. Fortunately, they still had lots of samosas for sale. Samosas are deep-fried triangles of pastry containing curried vegetables or meat.

"Could we have four of those samosas, please?" Mary Helen requested. "Where are you from?"

"Bombay," the matriarch responded. "But we live in Peterborough now."

"Um-m-m, delicious," I mumbled between bites. "Amazing to find Asian food at a farmer's market! Why don't you open up a shop in Cobourg or Port Hope? We are bereft of South Asian food there." I resurrected my rusty Urdu, which is akin to Hindi, to try it out on them. "Bahout mazedar!" (very tasty).

Their mouths fell open and their eyes lit up with astonishment. "Where did you learn to speak like that?" one queried.

After chatting about our years in Asia, we waved goodbye, promising to return again to get some curry.

A young father came toward us pulling a big red wagon divided into two sections. The first was heaped with vegetables and fruit. A giant cauliflower dominated the pile. In the back section a little boy and a girl were munching happily on huge cookies.

Seniors threaded their way through the throngs, buying produce for the week ahead. There were cottagers in town to vary their diet of dogs and burgers. Some wore designer shades and hats. Children ran in and out. Dogs on leashes sniffed the air as they sought the direction to the salami concession. Couples pushed strollers stuffed with children and produce. A long-haired throwback from the '60s, in beads, bangles, and earrings, pulled a cart piled with enough produce to feed a commune. Are there still communes? A family of vacationing Québécois wandered by. "Maman, nous allons manger de salade n'est ce pas?"

A clean-cut man in jeans and a checkered shirt paraded by with a sign held defiantly aloft. "Support your teachers now! Invest in quality education." It looked like we would have another autumn of strikes.

"Get away from my stall," shouted a man selling cheese from a specially constructed trailer." You teachers are already paid too much. No wonder my taxes are so high!"

Seeing a number of people in the throng nodding their agreement, the teacher beat a hasty retreat to a distant corner of the open-air market.

As we started up the next aisle I overheard a woman indignantly remark, as she stomped away from a vegetable stall, "Then it's not truly organic."

Curious, I wandered over to inquire about this organic skirmish. The leathery-faced farmer with the piercing blue eyes explained, "Oh, she asked me if my carrots were organic and I said 'yes.' The only fertilizer we use is manure from our cows. Then she asked me if we used antibiotics on the cows."

"Of course we do!" he huffed. "That's when she told me our manure was tainted and stomped off."

Not being organic purists ourselves, we bought some potatoes and cauliflower. Aside from the sign waver and a few organic purists, the mood of the crowd was mellow and cheerful.

Our next stop was a corner stall to buy some broccoli and corn. "Have you been coming to this market long?" I asked the couple tending the display.

"Oh, a good five years," the husband replied with a slight Dutch accent.

"Do you have the same spot every week?"

"We do now. It took us three years to get it though! At first we had to take whatever was left over. We were in a different spot every week. Now we have an assigned spot."

"Is it expensive to rent a spot?"

"We pay the city $500 a year for two table lengths—but that's good. It only comes to $20 a week through the season."

That would be twenty-five weeks, I reasoned. It seemed like a long time to come to an open-air market. "What do you sell when you don't have fresh vegetables?" I queried.

"In the spring I sell bedding plants and shrubs from my two greenhouses. We also sell vegetables that we store, like potatoes, onions, carrots and the like. If the weather is bad we have a stall over there in the building with the flea market."

"So, can you make a living from this?" I continued.

"We do okay. I had 300 cauliflower today. They're all gone. We've sold hundreds of heads of broccoli too. This is all we've got left. Oh, it's a good life. We like it. On Wednesdays we go to the downtown market as well."

We wandered until we discovered a big truck from the back of which some men from a First Nations community were selling wild blueberries. We can't resist blueberries—especially wild ones! They must have picked them in the rocky barrens to the north.

Our purchases complete, we sauntered over to the chip truck. Finding a shady spot we settled down to enjoy our chips and watch people wander by. According to a regular at the Guelph Farmers' Market, every market is dynamic, varying from week to week and from morning until noon when vendors pack up. Between 6:30 and 8:30 the grannies arrive. This over-90s club know quality and price better than any. "The grannies are a market's quality control." When they leave, the matrons arrive looking for "price, quantity and quality, in that order. They give you bonus points for dependable, fast service. The matrons really aren't much fun. Still, they are the economic backbone of the market."[112]

At 9:30 parents arrive with their children to enjoy an outing. Things become relaxed and friendly as curious children wander here and there. As the families leave, students come to buy their bread, cheese, veggies, and fruit. Things droop as the students leave and the bargain hunters prowl. As the market shuts down, "the tourists, still sleepy and somehow out of place, gawk in disappointment at the vendors who have begun to pack up."[113]

A century ago, visiting the market was the highlight of the week. Every city had one, as all those avenues named "Market Street" testify. Those streets are now market-less, lined instead with towers of glass and steel. Here and there a few, like the St. Lawrence Market in Toronto, struggle to survive the wrecking ball. Fortunately, in towns all over the western world, they are coming back. In 1973 Alberta had only four. By 1978 there were over sixty-five. Ontario had sixty-three by 1981, of which thirty-seven were open year round. Every Saturday, under the clock tower in Port Hope, farmers come to set up their stalls. At the same time others converge on the old Railway Station behind Victoria Hall in Cobourg. But the Peterborough Farmers' Market is the largest in our area and well worth a visit. Besides, the prices are reasonable, the produce is fresh, and one has the satisfaction of knowing that one is helping someone who appreciates the land.

Though we can't all live on the land, we have to keep a substantial proportion of us on it in order to re-establish and maintain our connection with it [since] most environmentalists tend to be urban.[114]

SORROW AND CELEBRATION

Trauma on Trespass Road

They would not spare the ancient oak
from feelings of veneration,
nor look upon it with regard
for any thing but its use as timber.
They have not time, even if they possessed the taste,
to gaze abroad on the beauties of Nature,
but their ignorance is bliss. [115]

On a lazy August morning in 1998, an array of alien sounds frazzled the fringes of my consciousness. Quietness is one of country living's most precious boons. Out here sustained noise signals something unusual. There is no drone of traffic, no honking of horns, no screeching of brakes, no whine of air conditioners. Sound is usually modulated and natural—the whisper of the wind, the hum of bees, the song of birds, the bawling of a heifer. Occasionally we hear the growl of a tractor or combine, the sound of Sandy's car as she delivers the mail, a lawnmower on a distant lawn, and once in a while, in winter, the whine of a passing snowmobile. But the harsh, sustained sound of machines at work is rare.

Could a farmer have begun his corn harvest early? Was a neighbour excavating a pond? Opening the front door, I listened. From over the hill to the north came the rumble of heavy machinery and the whine of chain saws. A new sign on the road urged caution: "Road Crew at Work." Assuming it signalled routine maintenance, I put it out of my mind and went back to work.

In the evening we set out on our regular walk. Duke ran to meet us. As we topped the rise at Randy and Kathi's place however, shock at the scene of devastation below stopped us in our tracks. A sign a hundred yards farther on warned, "Danger, Road Closed." A great earthmover, now silent, stood parked where it had begun to gouge flesh from a sandy hillock, home to our local colony of cliff swallows. The blade of a bulldozer rested on the pile of young saplings it had wrested from the soil. Beyond the dozer, a tangled mass of century-old pines and oaks lay bruised and bleeding where they had fallen. All of this was adjacent to an Eastern Bluebird sanctuary. We winced in sympathetic pain.

In one day our sylvan cathedral had been destroyed. One of the most attractive features of our patch of countryside had been the cloistered stretch of country road along which we routinely strolled with Duke. Giant pines, gnarled maples, black cherries, stalwart oaks, and black walnuts had been the columns defining the nave of our cathedral. Overhead an intricate tracery of branches had roofed in the nave sheltering us from the sun in summer and the winds of winter.

The vestments of our chapel changed with the seasons. The garb of autumn was skillfully woven from the rusty bronze of the red oaks, the vermilion of the white oaks, the yellow and crimson of the maples, and the hunter green of the pines. Winter changed its garb to ermine. Spring clothed the gothic splendour in the freshest, lightest tones of green. June and July saw it slip on the darker greens of summer that made it such a cool aisle to traverse.

Underneath the trees, a profusion of wild plants had carpeted the roadside. In spring, violets, trilliums, and columbines turned their faces to the sun. In summer, clumps of blackberry, waving grasses, Queen Anne's lace, and wild clover took over. Early autumn brought the asters and goldenrod.

The day after our initial shock, I went down and asked the supervisor, "What's happening?"

"We're widening and straightening the road," he replied.

"But why? This is not a through road. It's not even a very important road."

"We've had complaints that it's dangerous to drive. It's too narrow and hilly. A school bus and a car almost crashed at that hillock there. Farm machinery can hardly drive along it. Plus every year the township allocates money to improve one road."

"But why can't you leave the trees? Why are you bulldozing so far back?"

"Requirement. Whenever roads are improved, provincial guidelines require us to clear everything back 66 feet. There has to be a clear line of sight," he explained rather defensively.

"But we didn't hear anything about this. There was no public meeting," I rejoined.

"Not required," he said a little defensively. "The immediate neighbours were notified."

Much saddened, I left behind the whine of chain saws and the grumble of the dozer to head home. I'm sure he was surprised by my lack of enthusiasm for neighbourhood "improvement." I learned later that three of the four neighbours concerned, lamented the destruction of the trees as much as we.

How could this happen? In Toronto a million-dollar deal has been held up for years over two century-old white oaks.[116] It seems ironic that just when many urban gardeners are replacing weed-free lawns with "natural" gardens full of wildflowers, some country townships seem bent on sanitizing their roadscapes.

Over a period of a month or so, our country lane was cleared, scoured, gouged, burnt, straightened, and leveled. It was domesticated, sanitized, civilized, citified. The loggers cleared the road allowance of every tree—well over 400. Sawlogs disappeared. Hardwood logs unfit for lumber were stacked in great piles in neighbouring farmer's fields for them to use as firewood. Saplings and brush, and giant pines with any defect, were gathered into great piles and set on fire. Except for the few I salvaged, the century-old pine stumps that pioneers had used for their fences were added to the fires. The dozer scoured the road allowance bare of every wildflower, every sapling, every blackberry bush. The earthmover flattened the hillock and filled the gentle swales with raw earth. Trucks full of gravel laid down a new roadbed.

Without local consultation, marching to a drumbeat from some bureaucrat, a road crew had turned a country lane of rare charm into a flat, straight, uninteresting road to nowhere. The gentle undulations that wandered, ever so slightly, over hillock and dale had been domesticated to service the goddess "Speed." When completed (which took a further two years) our road stretched straight as an arrow, barren of vegetation, almost as level as a soccer field from Randi and Kathy's for 2 kilometres to its ending at the next concession.

Instead of a country road reflecting the character of the place, we ended up with a concession just like a thousand others—at a cost of well over $100,000. True, now we can see approaching cars and travel at break-neck speed. Small price, you say, to pay for safety and speed? Selfish, you say, to sacrifice "progress" on the altar of aesthetics?

But why couldn't the few who drive along our road have continued to exercise caution as drivers do along Britain's country lanes? Why couldn't they have reigned in the speed demon for a few minutes? Why couldn't the money have been spent on better schooling or health care? Or why couldn't they have compromised and widened it slightly, while maintaining the roadside flora? Trespass Road is a feeder road, not a highway. Only three kilometres long, it carries no through traffic, services ten houses and two working farms. "L" shaped, it begins at a main road and ends at a small concession.

I lament the vision that sees beauty not in the plants and trees along our roadways but in the technology that enables us to speed past scenery to scenic destinations. Part of the joy of rural life is found in traveling country roads. The enjoyment is as much in the travel as in the task to be accomplished at the destination. Ironically, this is the very problem addressed by a workshop I attended on maintaining and enhancing the natural beauty of roadsides throughout the township. I guess that workshop was another exercise in futility.

In his photo essay on our vanishing countryside, Ron Brown captures what remains, while arguing for more careful stewardship of our landscape. He points out that in our distant past many municipalities paid farmers up to 25 cents a tree to plant windbreaks along roads. He comments:

> *Few of those shady lines of trees remain, as the dictates of the auto age meant wider roads, and longer site lines. Age, too, has taken its toll, as many of those trees have reached maturity and must be cut. A few communities are replanting but, sadly, these are a minority and much of Ontario's country roadscapes have become*

*barren and treeless.... Farm modernization, too, has seen fields
widened and fences removed or replaced with the more recent
electrical fence. All have taken their toll on the country road.*[117]

Years ago Aldo Leopold in his classic work, *A Sand County
Almanac*, lamented the destruction of the native prairie of Wis-
consin. Every July he watched for the blooming of the compass
plant in a neglected corner of a local graveyard. This man-high
plant with saucer-sized yellow blooms resembling sunflowers
must have been spectacular—especially when a thousand acres
"tickled the bellies of the buffalo." Those that bloomed in the
graveyard seemed to be the only ones left in the western half of
his county. Then a road crew came, removed the fence and
straightened the road. Gone was the compass plant, probably
never to rise again.[118]

Leopold goes on to comment:

*Farm neighborhoods are good in proportion to the poverty of
their floras. My own farm was selected for its lack of goodness
and its lack of highway; indeed my whole neighborhood lies in
a backwash of the River of progress.*[119]

As a pastime he tabulated the number of wild plant species
blooming in suburbs and on the university farms as compared
to those on a backward farm. The result—120 versus 226. He
concludes:

*It is apparent that the backward farmer's eye is nearly twice as
well fed as the eye of the university student or businessman....
The shrinkage of flora is due to a combination of clean-farm-
ing, woodlot grazing, and good roads.... None of them requires,
or benefits by, the erasure of species from whole farms, townships, or counties. There are idle spots on every farm, and every
highway is bordered by an idle strip as long as it is; keep cow,*

plow, and mower out of these idle spots, and the full native flora plus dozens of interesting stowaways from foreign parts, could be part of the normal environment of every citizen.[120]

Occasionally in our travels we have noticed signs reading "No spraying," or "No mowing between signs." We never quite understood their urgent message until Progress destroyed the

Beginning of devastation on Trespass Road

beauty of our country road. Now we empathize. To even begin to slow this juggernaut will require a considerable realignment of values to enable us to treasure roadscapes, value bio-diversity, and enjoy the beauty of wild things.

Fortunately, like everything else in life, the trauma on Trespass Road had its positive side effects. A year later, we did get firewood at a reasonable price from one of the farmers bordering the destruction. And since we had to take more care in planning our walks, we ranged farther afield. We couldn't just walk out the door and down the road. We laid out a topographic map on the table and plotted sections of the Ganaraska Forest we had not hiked, concessions we had not traveled, unopened road allowances that might hide a trail, and unmaintained seasonal roads where traffic would be almost non-existent. In the course of the months that followed we discovered scores of, as yet, unspoiled country byways. On the map we marked each new roadway we explored with a yellow marker pen. We found new flowers. We saw deer and wild turkeys. And we left the dust and noise of the "road improvers" behind.

Sadly, Duke could not come with us on these jaunts. He frequently trotted over to our house to find out what kept us from our routine. We took him on short jaunts down the road away from the road crews. And then tragedy struck again. Duke became the victim of his own penchant for chasing cars. He was killed. Randy & Kathi's children were devastated, as were we. Duke had been a part of our country experience since the day we moved from the city. We would fiercely miss his friendliness, his loyalty, and his warm brown eyes.

Six years into our country adventure grief and disappointment played a requiem to innocence lost. But we discovered that those elements of country life that had endeared it to us were still there. The seasons still marched by. Gary still knew where the deer were yarding. Sandy still delivered the mail. Lev still worked the fields. His cattle still bawled for feed. And, very quickly, Queen Anne's lace and wild clover and black-eyed Susans began to invade the carefully manicured road allowance along Trespass Road.

Mechanized man, oblivious of flora, is proud of his progress in cleaning up the landscape on which, willy-nilly, he must live out his days. It might be wise to prohibit at once all teaching of real botany and real history, lest some future citizen suffer qualms about the floristic price of his good life.[121]

Celebration at Arrowhead Point

The spacious firmament on high,
With all the blue, ethereal sky,
And spangled heaven, a shining frame,
Their great Original proclaim:
Th' unwearied sun, from day to day,
Does his Creator's power display;
And publishes to every land
The work of an almighty hand.[122]

Although golden rod and asters fringed the concessions, summer's garb was frayed. The wheat harvest was long past. Soybeans and corn waited their turn. Ahead of us lay the golden days of autumn.

On a Sunday morning in September, seventy or eighty of us sat in lawn chairs under towering pines. Conversations were desultory, as if we were mesmerized by the beauty of the scene spread out before us. Streamers of mist clung to one of the islands like a wind-blown scarf. Mist hid the opposite shore. Sunshine, however, sparkled off the rippled surface of the water. Vacationers, beckoned back to the city by duty and commerce, had abandoned the lake to its year-round residents. The roar of outboards and jet skis had been silenced. Tranquility reigned. We breathed deeply of the scented air and drank in the quietness.

Late comers in a battered Ford pickup rattled into the clearing. They quietly tiptoed over to where we sat in the back row and spread their lawn chairs in the empty space to our left. "This space not taken is it?" queried a weathered old timer in a clean, starched white shirt that had begun to show signs of wear.

"No. Help yourself—and good morning," I replied. Then I recognized them. They were the couple who periodically rattled down Trespass Road at a crawl.

"I'm Eric and this is Mary Helen," I said.

"Oh, we know who you are," Clarence replied quietly, "You live in that log affair where the road jogs. I'm Clarence MacGregor and this is Mae."

Burning with curiosity, I could hardly restrain myself from probing further, but just then a young guitar player stood to welcome us. We had gathered from many denominations for a community church service in the open air.

A gentle breeze ruffled his auburn hair as he led us in the first hymn. There seemed nothing incongruous about a guitar accompaniment to a melody from Beethoven's Ninth Symphony as we lifted our voices to sing one of my favourites:

Joyful, joyful, we adore Thee,
God of glory, Lord of love:
Hearts unfold like flowers before Thee,
Opening to the sun above.
Melt the clouds of sin and sadness,

Drive the dark of doubt away;
Giver of immortal gladness,
Fill us with the light of day.[123]

I squeezed Mary Helen's hand as I gazed upward through the tracery of pine needles to the blue sky beyond. My mind wandered a bit as I thought back over the eight years since our move to Hemlock Meadow. We had rediscovered the sky and come to love the changing of the seasons. We had endured storms and critters, financial crises and struggles with stubborn wood stoves. And like people everywhere, we had agonized in helpless grief during times of darkness when friends had been stricken with cancer.

But where others saw all nature "red in tooth and claw" we had found our wounded spirits often restored through what we saw through our country window. Singing echoed through the grove:

All Thy works with joy surround Thee,
Earth and heaven reflect Thy rays,
Stars and angels sing around Thee,
Center of unbroken praise.
Field and forest, vale and mountain,
Flowery meadow, flashing sea,
Chanting bird and flowing fountain,
Call us to rejoice in Thee.[124]

I glanced around at our singing neighbours. Some I knew, some I didn't. Nevertheless, I felt a country kinship. A few were farmers with family trees rooted in country soil. Many, however, had made lifestyle decisions to deliberately embrace country living. On the far side Randy and Kathi sat with their growing family. They had chosen to bring up their children where there was space to stretch and horses to ride. The Wainwrights had left six-figure jobs on Bay Street to run a web-design business from their chalet overlooking Rice Lake. Ray and Audrey had retired to a bungalow on a hill with a view of the Northumberland Hills on one side and Lake Ontario on the other.

A lay preacher rose to speak. Turning down a lucrative offer from a Markham clinic, Howard had joined a family practice in Northumberland, in order to bring up his brood of four sons in a small town setting. In his rich voice he pointed to the scenery around us and declared, "Every Christian should be a naturalist!" He paused before continuing. "Why? Let me give you several reasons. We should be naturalists, first of all, because God wants us to enjoy what He has created. Paul wrote that we are to put our hope in God 'who richly provides us with everything for our enjoyment.'[125] Can you imagine a world without trees or flowers, mountains or lakes? It is because of the enjoyment we all find in the natural world that every weekend sees the highways out of Toronto clogged with cars.

"Secondly, nature provides a setting that encourages thought. Moses received the Ten Commandments on a mountain in the wilderness. David wrote his greatest Psalms while watching sheep or meditating in the desert. Nature has inspired the creativity of some of the world's greatest inventors, thinkers, and engineers. The famous Canadian inventor, Alexander Graham Bell, said, 'Don't keep forever on the public road. Leave the beaten track occasionally and dive into the woods. You will be certain to find something that you have never seen before, and before you know it you will have something worth thinking about to occupy your mind. All really big discoveries are the result of thought.'[126]

"Besides encouraging thought, nature inspires art. Seneca wrote that 'All art is imitation of nature.' The universe is a gallery in which are hung an infinite range of artistic works—a gallery that is never static. It presents an endless spectrum of textures, tints, and forms. Consider the pine needles fluttering in the breeze over our heads, the acorns at our feet, the milkweed parachutes drifting on the breeze, the clouds, the sunset, the stars, the flight of the hawk over the lake, the path of the bass beneath it, your fingers and mine.

"But there is another reason we ought to be naturalists. Given the value of this natural laboratory, we all need to be committed to its preservation. Jack Miner, father of conservation in Canada, has led the way. His banding program enabled him to solve many mysteries of migration. The foundation he began is credited with helping establish 200 bird sanctuaries in North America. Noting his use of words like pollution and conservation years before they became popular, the London Times commented that he lived fifty years ahead of his time. Of course, Jack Miner knew the source of all this. He wrote:

The Lord is my Guide and Teacher,
I will not get lost:
He makes my heart a receiving station for His wireless:
He sits down beside me in the pathless woods
and opens up his book of knowledge:
He turns the leaves very slowly that my dimmed eyes
may read His meaning.

He makes the trees I plant to grow,
and flowers to arch my path with their fragrant beauty;
gives me dominion over the fowls of the air
and they honk and sing their way to and from my home.

Yea, He has brought me up from a barefooted
underprivileged boy to a man respected by
millions of people, and I give Him all
the credit and praise whenever, wherever, and forever.[127]

"Finally, as Miner pointed out, creation inspires amazement and thanksgiving. John Muir founded the Sierra Club, a powerful force for ecological responsibility. Once, when Muir was standing with a friend at a high point of the Yosemite Valley, tears began to course down his cheeks. His friend was one of those rather unemotional types. Muir turned to him and, in the Scotch dialect into which he often lapsed when filled with wonder, said; 'Mon, can ye see unmoved the glory of the Almighty?'

"'Oh, it's very fine,' came the reply 'but I do not wear my heart upon my sleeve.'

"'Ah, my dear mon,' Muir replied, 'in the face of such a scene as this, it's no time to be thinkin' o' where you wear your heart.'[128]

"Muir was right. I hope our hearts are tender this morning—overwhelmed with amazement at the skill of the Creator, but moved to go beyond reading creation to devour His love letter, the Bible, in order to rediscover the wonderful story of Jesus."

As Howard sat down, the young guitarist rose to lead us in a concluding hymn:

This is my Father's world,
And to my listening ears
All nature sings, and round me rings
The music of the spheres.

This is my Father's world:
I rest me in the thought
Of rocks and trees, of skies and seas—
His hand the wonders wrought.[129]

Surreptitiously wiping away a tear that had trickled down my cheek, I turned to Clarence. "I think I've seen you driving by in your truck. Do you live near us?"

"Oh, we live in the village now," he replied so softly that I had to strain to hear him. "We used to live several concessions over from your place."

"Did you own a farm?"

"We had a hundred acres but lost it a few years ago. We live with my daughter now."

"Oh, that's too bad," I mumbled.

"God has taken care of us. Anyway, it got to be too much for us. Our oldest son was killed when a belt came loose on our thresher." Clarence screwed up his face at the memory. "Our youngest son didn't want the bother. He took computers and got a job in the city."

"That's sad. Must be hard to lose your land."

"Rough. Home farm… Grew up there… Married there. My granddad cleared the land. What can you do? Big corporations are taking over the farms."

No wonder he and his wife drive around the back roads at such a slow pace—remembering another time, checking up on what's happened to his land.

Everyone began to break open their picnic lunches and

spread them out, potluck style, on several picnic tables. Over ham sandwiches and coleslaw we continued to chat with Clarence and Mae.

"Wonderful to have this service," Mae commented. "We used to take turns having services on our front lawn in the summer. No church building then. Just a preacher with a four-point charge."

As we bid our new friends goodbye, I asked, "Can we invite you over for coffee some afternoon? We'd love to hear more about what this township was like when you were younger."

"Oh, I don't know. I doubt if we'll last much longer."

"Clarence!" Mae scolded, "You're as healthy as a filly in oats. Sure we'll come. We appreciate the invitation."

As we waved goodbye, Mary Helen and I glanced at each other and smiled. Here were two people who really knew the country roads around Hemlock Meadow. In the days ahead, their shared memories would enable us to develop a whole new appreciation for the scenes we see from day to day through our country window.

Endnotes

NOTE: *"CQP" denotes a quotation cited in the Dictionary of Canadian Quotations and Phrases (CQP), Toronto: McClelland and Stewart, 1982.*

"Bartlett's" denotes, John Bartlett, Bartlett's Familiar Quotations, Boston & Toronto: Little, Brown and Company, 15th edition, 1980.

---

1 William Shakespeare, *Measure for Measure*, Act I, Scene IV, line 78.

2 Joseph Wood Krutch, *The Desert Year*, Toronto: George J. McLeod, 1951, pp. 4-5.

3 William Browne, *Variety*, (1591-1643).

4 Helen Keller.

5 André Picard, *Giving a damn*, The Toronto Star, November 15, 1997, pp. C1.

6 McNight, John, *The Careless Society: Community And Its Counterfeitsü* (cited by Picard, *Giving a damn*, The Toronto Star, Nov. 15, 1997, p.C4).

7 David McCord, *Ballade of Time and Space*, 1935 (839:3, Bartlett's).

8 Chuck Shepherd, *News of the Weird*, The Toronto Star, Oct. 25, 1997.

[9] Bob Weber, *Prairies are going hog wild*, The Toronto Star, Oct. 25, 1997, E6.

[10] Ralph Waldo Emerson, *Nature*, A Facsimile of the First Edition with introduction by Jaroslave Pelikan, Boston: Beacon Press, 1985, p. 9,10.

[11] Ibid, p. 54.

[12] Walt Whitman, *When I Heard the Learn'd Astronomer* cited in *The Sierra Club Nature Writing Handbook*, John A. Murray, ed., San Francisco: Sierra Club Books, 1995, p. 123.

[13] A paraphrase of Psalm 19, vs. 1-6: Eugene H. Peterson, *The Message—Psalms*, Colorado Springs: Navpress, 1994, p.27.

[14] Proverbs 27:10.

[15] George Herbert, *Jacula Prudentum* [1651] No. 49.

[16] Emily G. Murphy, ("Janey Canuck"), *Open trails*, 1912, p. 116.

[17] Peter Mayle, *A Year in Provence*, New York: Knopf, 1990, p. 6.

[18] Jean Whitman, "Kinship", 1938, cited in CQP, p. 616.

[19] Ralph Waldo Emerson, *Nature*, p. 53.

[20] Sherrell Branton Leetooze, *Built on Faith and Fortitude: A brief history of Hope Township, Bowmanville, Ontario*, Lynn Michael-John Associates, 1997.

[21] Henry David Thoreau, *Thoreau: Walden and Other Writings*, Bantam compendium, New York: 1962, p. 108.

[22] Peter McArthur, *In pastures green*, 1915, p. 93, cited in CQP, p. 342.

[23] Proverbs 6:6-11.

[24] Psalm 127:2.

25 Archibald Lampman, "The child's music lesson", 1888, cited in CQP, p. 577.

26 Proverbs 17:6a.

27 Thomas Moore, *National Airs [1815] Oft in the Stilly Night*, st. I, Bartlett's, p. 447.

28 Isabella Valancy Crawford, *Malcolm's Katie*, 1884.

29 See Euell Gibbons, *Stalking The Wild Aspargus*, New York: David McKay, 1962, Field Guide Edition reprint 1974, p. 90.

30 Thomas Wentworth Higginson (1823-1911).

31 William W. Campbell, *Indian Summer*, 1889, cited in CQP p. 92.

32 Theodore Agrippa D'Augbigné (1552-1630), *Les Tragiques. Les Feux*, Bartlett's, p. 171.

33 Lynn Johnston, *For Better or For Worse*, The Toronto Star, Oct. 11, 1997.

34 Emerson, *Nature*, p. 19.

35 Robert Service, 1907.

36 Aldo Leopold, *A Sand County Almanac*, foreword, 1949.

37 Dr. Robin Baker, contributing editor, *The Mystery of Migration*, Toronto: Wiley, 1980, p. 135.

38 Joe Van Warmer, *The World of the Canada Goose*, Philadelphia & New York: J. B. Lippincott, 1968, p. 25.

39 Kit Howard Breen, *The Canada Goose*, Vancouver/Toronto: 1990, p. 4.

40 Robert Bateman, *The Art of Robert Bateman*, Toronto: Madison Press Books, 1981, p.66.

41 Quoted from Sir Peter Scott, by Kit Howard Breen, *The Canada Goose*, Vancouver/Toronto: 1990, p. 4.

[42] Anonymous, cited in Harrowsmith Country Life, October 1997, p. 11.

[43] Percy Bysshe Shelley, *Ode to the West Wind*, 1819.

[44] Georges Simenon, *November*, New York: Hamish Hamilton Ltd. & Harcourt Brace Jovanovich, Inc., English translation, 1970.

[45] John Burroughs, *Is It Going To Rain*, 1877.

[46] Wilson, MacDonald, "A poet stood forlorn", 1918, cited in CQP, p. 950.

[47] Jennie E. Haight, "Snow", in Dewart, *Selections*, 1864, 132, cited in CQP.

[48] R. D. Lawrence, *The Place in the Forest*, North Vancouver: J.J. Douglas Ltd., 1974 edition, pp. 93,94.

[49] Anonymous saying of pioneer Ontario farmers cited in CQP, p. 837.

[50] Alexander McLauchlan, "The Emigrant", 1861.

[51] Inscription over an early fireplace in Lower Canada, cited in CQP p. 434.

[52] Maxine Hancock, *Living On Less & Liking It More*, Chicago: Moody Press, 1976, p. 125.

[53] Matthew 6:25-34.

[54] Henry Thoreau, *Walden*, pp.16, 24.

[55] Charles Dickens, *A Christmas Carol*, 1843.

[56] Albert D. Watson, *Christmas*, 1914.

[57] Lawrence, *The Place in the Forest*, pp. 72,73.

[58] James Gay, *Canadian climate*, cited in CQP, p. 963.

[59] Wilfred Campbell, "Under the wild witchery of the winter woods", 1922, cited in CQP, p. 364.

60 Emerson, *Nature*, p. 23.

61 Peter McArthur, "Birds of passage", 1907 cited in CQP, p. 107.

62 Lawrence, p. 66.

63 Ibid, p. 67.

64 Francis Rye, *Canadian Birthday Book*, 1887, p. 384, cited in CQP, p. 963.

65 John Donne, "Verse Letter to Sir Henry Wotton", before April 1598, cited in Bartletts, p. 254.

66 Anonymous, cited in William J. Bennet, editor, *The Book of Virtures*, New York: Simon & Schuster, 1993, p. 330.

67 William E. Marshall, *Brookfield*, 1914, cited CQP, p. 856.

68 Bliss Carman, "Spring song", 1894, cited CQP, p. 856.

69 Susanna Moodie, *Roughing It in the Bush*, 1852, cited in CQP, p. 564.

70 From "Maple Syrup: History of the Industry", http://www.maple-erable.qc.ca/history.html; 07/10/2000.

71 Arthur S. Bourinot, *Sugar Bush*, 1951 cited in CQP p. 566.

72 Archibald Lampman, "Hepaticas".

73 Rudyard Kipling, "The Flowers", 1895, cited in CQP, p. 355.

74 Robert Service, "Trees against the sky", 1940, cited in CQP, 903.

75 Quoted by John Langton in Wallace, University of Toronto, 1927, p. 75, cited in CQP, p. 903.

76 Catharine P. Traill, *Backwoods of Canada*, 1836, p. 154, cited in CQP, p. 903.

77 Anna B. Jameson, *Winter Studies and Summer Rambles*,

1838, Vol. 3, p. 96; cited in CQP, p. 903.

[78] Catharine Parr Traill, *Pearls and Pebbles*, 1894, p. 134, cited in CQP, p. 903.

[79] Algernon Charles Swinburne, *Atalanta in Calydon*, 1865, st. 4.

[80] Bliss Carman, "Over the wintry threshold", Smart Set, April 1913.

[81] Ben Jonson, cited in *The Book of Virtues*, p. 431.

[82] Andrew (J.R.) Ramsay, "Atkinson's mill", 1880, cited in CQP, p. 583.

[83] Proverb quoted in Chaucer, *The Canterbury Tales*, Prologue, line 563.

[84] Duncan Campbell Scott, "Spring on Mattagami", 1916, cited in CQP, p. 857.

[85] Anne Wilkinson, "Letter to my children", in contemporary verse, Fall-Winter, 1952, cited in CQP, p.822.

[86] George Herbert, "Virtue", stanzas 1 & 3, 1633, cited in Bartlett's, p. 268.

[87] Emerson, *Nature*, p. 21.

[88] Jack Lessinger, *Penturbia*, Seattle: SocioEconomics Inc., 1991, title page.

[89] Paul Hiebert, *Sarah Binks,* "My Garden", 1947, p. 12, cited in CPQ, p. 391.

[90] Term used by Robertson Davies for his fictional character Samuel Marchbanks, in the Peterborough Examiner in the 1940s.

[91] Genesis 2: 8,9,15.

[92] Revelation 22:2,3.

[93] Dan Needles, "The Diner in the Village", cited in Har-

rowsmith Country Life, June 2000, p.122.

94 Proverbs 30: 24-28.

95 Archibald Lampman, "The wind's word", Independent, July 26, 1894, cited CPQ, p.960.

96 Third Recitation, Haydn's Oratorio, "The Creation".

97 Andrew J. Ramsay, "Win-on-ah", 1869, cited CQP, p. 950.

98 Cited in the University Bulletin, University of Alberta, Alfred M. Rehwinkel, *The Wonders of Creation*, Minneapolis: Bethany, 1974, p. 85.

99 Ibid, p. 80, cited from Natural History, New York: The Museum of Natural History, April, 1968, p. 31.

100 Ibid, cited from the Press Bulletin, University of Alberta, Dec. 26, 1930.

101 Almanac, "Country Sightings", Montreal: Harrowsmith Country Life, August 1997, p. 9.

102 Job 36:26-30; 37:2-4.

103 Song written for the 4th Line Theatre production, *The Orchard*, Robert Winslow and Ian McLachlan, Millbrook, Ontario.

104 From the 4th Line Theatre's 1998 summer program.

105 Ibid.

106 Sharon Butala, *The Perfection of the Morning*, Toronto: HarperCollins, 1994, p. 179.

107 Butala, pp. 179, 180.

108 Butala, p. 178.

109 Jean Blewett, "The firstborn", 1922.

110 Kenneth McNeill Wells, *The Owl Pen*, Toronto: Stoddart, 1995, p. 38.

111 From the article by Jacqueline Johnson, *Confessions of the Zucchini Lady*, Camden East, Ontario: Harrowsmith, June/July 1981, p. 59.

112 Ibid.

113 Ibid.

114 Butala, pp. 180, 181.

115 Catherine Parr Traill, *Backwoods of Canada*, 1836, p. 154, cited in CQP, p. 903.

116 Jim Rankin, "How two old oaks have embroiled city in a 3-year legal battle", Toronto Star, July 30, 2000, p. A1.

117 Ron Brown, *Disappearing Ontario*, Toronto: Polar Bear Press, 1999, p. 95,97.

118 Aldo Leopold, *A Sand County Almanac*, New York: Ballantine, 1970, p. 49.

119 Ibid, p. 50.

120 Ibid, p. 51.

121 Ibid, p. 50.

122 *The Spacious Firmament*, text by Joseph Addison, based on Psalm 19; music by Franz Joseph Haydn.

123 Text of "Joyful, Joyful, We Adore Thee" by Henry van Dyke: music by Ludwig van Beethoven; melody from Ninth Symphony; adapted by Edward Hodges.

124 Ibid.

125 1 Tim. 6:17.

126 Cited by R.D. Lawrence in *Where Water Lilies Grow*, Toronto: Natural Heritage/Natural History Inc., 1999, p. 206.

127 From *Jack Miner: Father of Conservation*, undated paper printed by The Trustees of the Jack Miner Foundation.

128 Sierra, March/April 1989, p. 23.

129 *This Is My Father's World*, text by Maltbie D. Babcock, music by Franklin L. Sheppard.

Order Form

If you are unable to purchase *Through a Country Window* from your local bookstore send your order by mail or fax as indicated below (please print):

By Mail: Wildwood Writing Service
RR #1, Campbellcroft, ON
L0A 1B0 Canada

By Fax: Wildwood Writing Service
905-797-2490

Payment: Canadian $18.95 per copy
US $13.95 per copy

Shipping: Include $2.50 per book for shipping and handling. Books will be sent surface mail unless otherwise arranged.

✂ -

Please send me _____ copies of *Through a Country Window*. I have enclosed a cheque or money order for _____ (made payable to Wildwood Writing Service) including $2.50 per book to cover shipping and handling by surface mail.

Name: _____

Address:_____

City: _____

Prov./State: _____ Postal/Zip Code _____

Telephone: _____ **E-mail:** _____